4
5
36

FOUNDATIONS OF MODERN ECONOMICS SERIES

Otto Eckstein, *Editor*

FOUNDATIONS OF MODERN ECONOMICS SERIES

OTTO ECKSTEIN *Harvard University*

Public Finance

THIRD EDITION

PRENTICE-HALL, INC. *Englewood Cliffs, New Jersey*

Library of Congress Cataloging in Publication Data

ECKSTEIN, OTTO.
    Public Finance.

    (Foundations of modern economics series)
    Bibliography: p.
    1. Finance, Public—United States. I. Title.
HJ257. E25 1973   336. 73   72-8812
ISBN 0-13-737460-7
ISBN 0-13-737478-X (pbk.)

PRENTICE-HALL FOUNDATIONS
OF MODERN ECONOMICS SERIES

Otto Eckstein, *Editor*

10 9 8 7 6 5 4 3 2 1

PRENTICE-HALL INTERNATIONAL INC., *London*
PRENTICE-HALL OF AUSTRALIA, PTY., LTD., *Sydney*
PRENTICE-HALL OF CANADA, LTD., *Toronto*
PRENTICE-HALL OF INDIA PVT. LIMITED, *New Delhi*
PRENTICE-HALL OF JAPAN, INC., *Tokyo*

Foundations

of Modern Economics Series

Economics has grown so rapidly in recent years, it has increased so much in scope and depth, and the new dominance of the empirical approach has so transformed its character, that no one book can do it justice today. To fill this need, the Foundations of Modern Economic Series was conceived. The Series, brief books written by leading specialists, reflects the structure, content, and key scientific and policy issues of each field. Used in combination, the Series provides the material for the basic one-year college course. The analytical core of economics is presented in *Prices and Markets* and *National Income Analysis*, which are basic to the various fields of application. Two books in the Series, *The Evolution of Modern Economics* and *Economic Development: Past and Present*, can be read without prerequisite and can serve as an introduction to the subject.

The Foundations approach enables an instructor to devise his own course curriculum rather than to follow the format of the traditional textbook. Once analytical principles have been mastered, many sequences of topics can be arranged and specific areas can be explored at length. An instructor not interested in a complete survey course can omit some books and concentrate on a detailed study of a few fields. One-semester courses stressing either macro- or micro-economics can be readily devised. The instructors guide to the Series indicates the variety of ways the books in the Series can be used.

The books in the Series are also being used as supplements to the basic textbooks, to permit a fuller curriculum on some toipcs. Intermediate level courses are using volumes in the Series as the core text, and are combining it with various readings.

This Series is an experiment in teaching. The positive response to the first two editions has encouraged us to continue to develop and improve the approach. New books are being added and the previous books revised and updated. The thoughtful reactions of many teachers who have used the books in the past have been of immense help in preparing the third edition.

The books do not offer settled conclusions. They introduce the central problems of each field and indicate how economic analysis enables the reader to think more intelligently about them, to make him a more thoughtful citizen, and to encourage him to pursue the subject further.

Otto Eckstein, *Editor*

Contents

Public Finance

Government is big and important in our economic system. The American people rely on government to protect individual freedom, maintain social justice, supply public services, and to provide a system of laws that permits the free market economy to function. The quality of government goes a long way to determine the performance of the entire economy. If government is inefficient, resources are wasted and taxes are unnecessarily high. If government assumes too many functions, private performance deteriorates: households and businesses are no longer able to exercise their initiative effectively and to reach the rational, decentralized decisions that are essential for a properly functioning market economy. If government assumes too little responsibility, private economic power may be exercised in ways detrimental to the economy as a whole; disparities in income and wealth may become too great; and public services worthy of a great and wealthy country may not be provided.

This book is an introduction to public finance, the study of the revenue and expenditure activities of government. It discusses budgets, taxes, government expenditures, and public debts. Public finance is the study of the effects of budgets on the economy, particularly the effect on the achievement of the major economic objectives—growth, stability, equity, and efficiency. It is also the study of "what ought to be": Assuming that we wish to accomplish certain objectives such as increased growth or a fairer distribution of income, what specific policies will accomplish the objectives?

An understanding of public finance should help you grapple meaningfully with such key public issues as:

1. How wide should the scope of public activity be?
2. What is the proper level at which a public service should be performed—federal, state, or local?
3. Is our tax system threatening the growth of the economy?
4. Why have state and local governments fallen on such hard times? And how can they be helped without concentrating all control in Washington?
5. How can government best combat the business cycle, given the inevitable human failings of delay and occasional misjudgment?
6. Why should we be worried about the national debt?

This book will not settle these questions for you. You will have to add your own philosophical values, your view of human nature, and even a little of your own emotions—how you feel about government—to reach your own conclusions. But economics is a large part of the story, and you cannot make much headway in answering these questions unless you know something about it.[1]

[1] I am grateful to Harvey Brazer, Samuel M. Cohn, Martin David, Richard T. Gill, John Kuhlman, Joseph A. Pechman, and Nathan Rosenberg for helpful suggestions.

The Scope

of Government Activity

CHAPTER ONE

Ours is a capitalist economy. We rely on private enterprise to supply most of our economic wants. Yet government has grown enormously in size and in the variety of its activities. At the beginning of the century, government expenditures at all levels were only $1.6 billion or 8 percent of GNP; federal expenditures amount to just $500 million. There was no income tax.

By 1972, government expenditures exceeded $350 billion—31 percent of GNP. The economy had grown, too, but not so massively as government.

What accounts for these steep increases? First, the United States is one of the two great world powers and shoulders a heavy burden of military expenditures. Thirty-seven percent of all federal expenditures are devoted to defense, international programs and commitments, and space research; the cost of past wars—interest on the national debt and veterans' benefits—represents another 13 percent.

Second, government has taken responsibility for the welfare of those individuals who are unable to provide for themselves. In earlier times, each family had to care for its own aged, disabled, and widowed; and those hapless souls without families were forced to live on pitifully small doles amid miserable conditions. As the average life span lengthened and the traditional large family was fragmented into separate generations, income support became a public function. Today, social security, public assistance, and other income maintenance programs cost over $70 billion a year.

Third, people receive a lot more education to equip them to work and live in our technologically advanced society. Forty years ago, one-

3

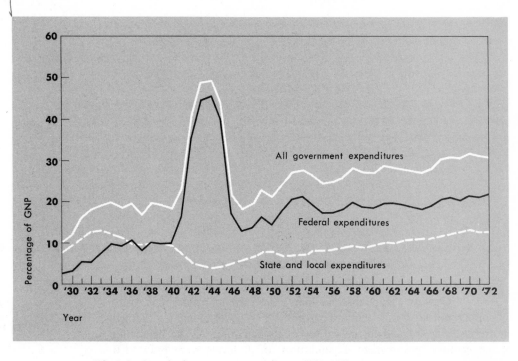

FIG. 1—1 Growth of government expenditures, 1929–1972.

third of all young people finished high school. Today, over two-thirds graduate, and those who do not must resign themselves to a lifetime of unskilled labor.

Fourth, the growth of population and the concentration of people in urban areas have led to greatly increased expenditures for transportation, sanitation, water supply, housing, and other public services. A farmer in the last century may have drawn his water from his well, fed his garbage to his pigs, protected his family with his rifle. His grandson in the city would be ill-advised to try to provide these services for himself.

Finally, rising costs have raised government's share in the economy. Most government expenditures are for services, such as education, health, fire and police protection, and sanitation. Productivity has not improved as much in these areas as in the economy as a whole. Although the pay of public employees lags at times, in the long run they receive about the same amounts and increments as other workers. As a result, the unit cost of these public services has increased steadily.

Economic development and rising incomes are accompanied everywhere by increased government functions. In little-developed countries such as Ethiopia or Afghanistan, government expenditures are only about 5 percent of total GNP. **4** In developing countries such as India and Pakistan, they are 10 percent; in Greece and Japan, about 20 percent. Nor is the United States, with its expenditure at 31 percent, at the top of the list. Sweden, West Germany, and France, which spend a great deal more than the U.S. on welfare programs, have ratios as high as 33 percent.

The ratio of government expenditures to gross national product is a very crude measure of the scope of government activity. Only some of the expenditures are *exhaustive*—that is, absorbing real resources from the economy through purchases of goods and services. The rest of the expenditures are *transfer payments*, such as the transfer of money to individuals for social security benefits, to businesses as subsidies, or to other governments as grants-in-aid. Table 1–2 reveals the recent trends.

Exhaustive expenditures divert resources into the public sector. Government decisions reached through the political process determine how this portion of the total output of the economy is to be used. Through transfer payments, on the other hand, government merely shifts purchasing power from one decision unit to another, with the recipient determining how the money is to be spent.

Nor are all exhaustive expenditures the result of direct government activity. Half represent government purchases of the products of private enterprises, such as missiles, food, or school buildings. They represent private production devoted to public uses. The other half do represent *government production*—that is, the labor of government employees such as soldiers, teachers, policemen, and firemen.

Centralization of power is one of the drawbacks of the growth of government expenditures, but this is a concern mainly related to the federal government. Federal expenditures are almost twice the size of total state and local expenditures, despite the more rapid recent growth at the state and local level. But the states and localities account for more than half of the exhaustive expenditures

Table 1–1 GOVERNMENT EXPENDITURES BY FUNCTION, 1971
(billions of dollars)

Federal		State and Local	
National defense	75.3	Education	59.2
Social security, medicare,		Highways	16.6
welfare, etc.	68.7	Public assistance	19.9
Interest	14.6	Health and hospitals	11.2
Veterans' benefits	11.3	Police	6.5
Transportation	7.8	Natural resources	3.5
Space	3.5	Sewers	3.0
Agriculture	5.7	Fire	2.6
Health research and hospitals	3.6	Prisons	2.1
International affairs	3.2	Other (administration, labor,	
Natural resources	3.7	regulation, agriculture, etc.)	22.4
Education	5.7		
Housing and community dev.	3.4		
Other (administration, postal			
service, labor, etc.)	14.3		
Total	220.8	Total	147.0

Source: National Income and Product Accounts, U.S. Department of Commerce.

Table 1–2 SIZE OF THE PUBLIC SECTOR, 1971
(billions of dollars)

	Federal	State and Local	Total
Expenditures	220.8	147.0	338.5
Exhaustive (purchases of goods and services)	97.8	135.0	232.8
Government employees	47.5	77.3	124.8
Purchases from business	50.2	57.7	107.9
Transfer payments	101.7	16.6	—
To persons	72.4	16.6	89.0
To state and local governments	29.3	—	—
Other (interest on debt; subsidies; current surplus of government enterprises (—); etc.)	21.3	−4.6	16.7
Receipts	199.1	151.8	—
Taxes and other own sources	199.1	122.5	321.6
Transfers from federal government	—	29.3	—
Surplus (+) or deficit (—)	−21.7	4.8	−16.9

* Net of transfers from federal to state and local governments to avoid double-counting.

Source: National Income and Product Accounts, U.S. Department of Commerce.

(see Table 1–2). They are responsible for most civilian public services, including education. Apart from its defense spending, the federal government is mainly a reshuffler of money—taxing on the one hand, transferring to individuals and state and local governments on the other.

No one numerical magnitude can fully reflect the importance of government in the economy. The level of taxes has its significance: each dollar of taxation, whether spent on exhaustive expenditures or transfers, represents a little bit of compulsion. It can affect private incentives and the growth of the economy. Furthermore, some government activities that cost practically nothing are extremely important. The numerous regulatory activities, the administration of justice, and the creation of new laws by the Congress and the president mold the institutional shape of the economy. Certainly, their dollar cost is no measure of their significance.

ARE THERE LAWS OF GROWTH OF GOVERNMENT SPENDING?

The German economist Adolph Wagner, writing in 1883, thought he had discovered the "Law of Ever-Increasing State Activity" upon surveying the public-expenditure records of several advanced countries in the nineteenth century. He based his "Law" on the "pressure for social progress and resulting changes in the relative spheres of private and public economy, especially compulsory public economy." History has certainly borne him out, although war and its aftermath have cost more than social progress.

Peacock and Wiseman[1] have tested Wagner's ideas with modern statistics for Britain. They found his "Law" still working, but they provide a rather more complicated explanation. They find that expenditures grow because revenues grow, rather than the other way about; a given tax system with constant tax rates yields more money as the economy grows, and governments, like most of us, somehow spend their income. Furthermore, the cost of providing public services grows with the nation. There is usually a substantial gap between people's desires for expenditures and their tolerance levels of taxation. The pressures for larger budgets are always immense. To the extent that revenues are available, the guardians of the public purse (the conservative politicians, budget bureaus, and treasuries of the world) have little power to refuse requests. Only when action is required to raise tax rates to finance new spending can they say "No!" and make it stick.

Besides this gradual growth of expenditures in line with revenues, every few decades the necessity to finance a war leads to a broadening of the tax system. Once the war is over, the system does not return to its prewar level; some of the new taxes are continued, so that the growth trend of revenues and expenditures is moved upward permanently. They call this movement the *displacement effect*.

The theory seems to fit fairly well for British experience. Does it apply equally to the United States? At best, in a rather general way. Tax rates at the federal level change only infrequently and in peacetime tend to move down. The displacement effect has occurred after recent wars, but can largely be explained by continued high military expenditures. State and local governments, on the other hand, that have not had the benefit of the displacement effect, have been forced to adopt new taxes and to raise rates steadily in the last 15 years as their costs have risen. Thus, although there inevitably is a lot of momentum in existing spending programs in a growing economy, long-term movements in expenditure levels are as much the result of conscious policy decisions by the president, the Congress, local governments, and, in the last analysis, by the voters.

DEFINING THE PROPER SCOPE
OF GOVERNMENT ACTIVITY

What is the proper scope of government? Are there economic criteria that can help us to decide whether an activity should properly be in the public or in the private sector? This question has concerned thinkers since ancient times. Adam Smith, founder of classical economics, confined the list to (1) defense, (2) the administration of justice, and (3) certain public works.[2] Today,

---

[1] Alan T. Peacock and Jack Wiseman, *The Growth of Public Expenditure in the United Kingdom* (Princeton, N.J.: Princeton University Press, 1961).

[2] Adam Smith, *The Wealth of Nations* (New York: The Modern Library, 1937), introduction to Book V.

three approaches to this question can be discerned: (1) permit government action only when the private sector cannot do the job; (2) permit a more active role for government; (3) the socialist approach.

Private enterprise, operating in a market economy, will meet most desires of consumers in an advanced country like ours. There are, however, some limited situations in which the market cannot function properly; then government takes some action. These situations have certain economic characteristics that cause the market mechanism to fail.

Collective goods. These are goods and services that simply cannot be provided through the market. They have two related qualities. First, they inevitably have to be supplied to a group of people rather than on an individual basis. Second, they cannot be withheld from individuals who refuse to pay for them.

Take national defense, for example. The national security provided by our military forces is extended to all persons in the country. They all receive the same protection, whether they are willing to pay for it or not. There is no way of withholding the service, of creating a market that separates those who pay from the freeloaders. In fact, in this type of situation, the rational, wholly self-interested consumer of economic theory will never pay because he will get the benefit in any event.[3]

In the case of ordinary private goods, this difficulty does not occur. If one person likes some item of food or clothing or a service, and another does not, one will pay for it and receive it, the other will not. If someone should refuse to pay yet wish to obtain the product, the sellers would simply refuse to give it to him. This crucial distinction has been called the *exclusion principle*: a good is *private* if someone who does not pay can be excluded from its use. If it cannot be withheld (violating the exclusion principle), it is a *collective* good.

Defense is not the only collective good. Other expenditures for foreign-policy objectives—foreign aid, space exploration, and so on—exhibit the same quality. Some domestic cases are flood control, where a dam protects all the persons in a valley whether each agrees to pay or not, police and fire protection, and the administration of justice. The examples tend to match Adam Smith's list.

Not all goods supplied jointly to many people are collective goods. In some instances, the exclusion principle applies. The services of a movie theater can be enjoyed by many people at about the same cost as by one; but the service is marketable because admission can be denied to those who refuse to pay. Roads and parks are on the borderline; sometimes they can be withheld, sometimes not.

Divergence between private and social costs or benefits. In order for pri-

8

---

[3] But notice that it is rational for him to cast his vote for defense expenditures plus the taxes to finance them. For then he will not have to pay unless everyone else is also compelled to pay through taxation.

vate decisions based on market prices to lead to the economically best result, prices must be sound indicators of social benefits and costs. In a well-working competitive market economy, prices reflect the relative values of different goods to consumers, as well as the marginal costs of producers, thus equating marginal values to consumers with the marginal costs of producers. Prices serve as a signaling device of benefits and costs. But in some situations, a private decision maker may not have to pay for all the costs he causes the economy; in others he may not be able to reap all the benefits. The prices he will be using in his decisions will not fully measure the true values to the economy as a whole; consequently, prices will cease to yield correct signals, and private decisions based on them will not produce an optimal result. These divergencies are sometimes called *external economies* or *diseconomies*.

For example, a paper mill that pollutes a river imposes a cost on society for which the mill is not charged. It reduces the value of the river to the economy, yet the mill will not consider this cost in its profit-maximizing calculations. Conversely, when Western Electric scientists invented the transistor, other companies, both in the U.S. and abroad, gained far more than any patent royalties they may have paid, not to mention the benefits to consumers.

Usually, these unrecompensed benefits and costs are minor and do not constitute sufficient cause for government intervention, much less government operation. Just because one corporation puts up an eyesore of a skyscraper while a more tasteful company beautifies the city with its headquarters, the one company is not penalized or the other rewarded. But sometimes the divergencies between the private and the public benefit-cost calculus become so great that the activity must fall within the scope of government. Here are two cases:

Figure 1–2 shows the economies of a typical storage reservoir in the West, which carries over water from wet seasons to dry and also from wet years to dry. When the water is released, it passes through twelve downstream dams, generating power at each one—in fact, three-fourths of the resultant power is developed downstream. A private company would not develop Hungry Horse; most of the benefit would accrue to other private power companies. The result: Hungry Horse is a public project.

But although government intervention was necessary, public ownership was not the only possible solution. A private company might have been given the legal power to collect a fee for the benefits it was providing to others; the federal government might have paid a private company a subsidy to compensate for the downstream benefits; a voluntary association of downstream beneficiaries might have been formed to put up the dam; or a mixed private-public setup could have been devised under which the federal government might have built the dam and left the power equipment to be provided by private enterprise. But in our society we do not like to pay subsidies to large companies, or to give private companies what amounts to the power to tax. And voluntary associations are not easy to organize when conflicting interests are involved. So, situations of this sort often lead to government operation.

A more important example is education. Everybody gains from living in a

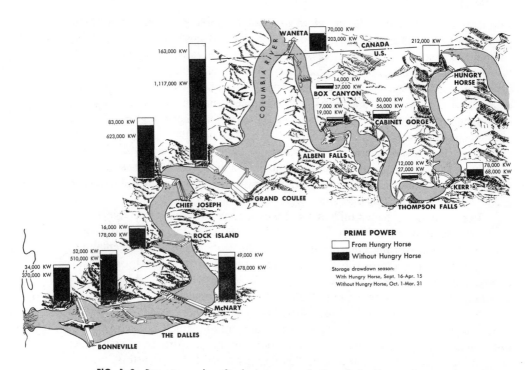

FIG. 1–2 Downstream benefits for power production of the Hungry Horse project. (Source: J. V. Krutilla and O. Eckstein, *Multiple Purpose River Development*, Baltimore: Johns Hopkins Press, 1958, p. 63. Adapted from chart published by Bonneville Power Administration.)

democracy with an educated citizenry. Also, some of the economic benefit of having an educated labor force accrues to employers through lower production costs and to consumers through lower prices, although it is impossible to determine precise amounts. Here, too, there is a choice of method of intervention. Schools could be public, or parents could be given subsidies to pay tuition in private schools. To assure attendance, reliance could be placed on the incentive of future returns and social custom, or it could be made compulsory. The U.S. has chosen public operation and compulsion up to a certain age.

Extraordinary technological risks. Although private enterprise thrives on risk-taking, some types of risk can be shouldered only by government. For example, private companies could not develop atomic energy as a source of electric power. The total research cost was enormous; a number of years had to pass before production costs were brought down to economical levels; and even if one of our corporate giants had been willing to take the huge risk, it would not have reaped the full benefit; it could not be given a patent monopoly that would have recouped its investment. Thus, heavy technological risk was compounded because the benefits could not be fully appropriated by the risk-taker. Two forms of intervention have been used in such situations: direct government activity

10

(for example, government laboratories such as Los Alamos and Huntsville), or more commonly, government contracts to private industry (as in the development of giant computers, supersonic airliners, and most space work).

Natural monopolies. The supply of electricity, gas, telephone service, and mass transportation usually is carried out most effectively if a single organization provides the service in a community. Average costs fall with size, and if two or more companies compete, they may have to provide wasteful duplicate facilities. Thus, a monopoly is typically the most efficient supplier. But without competition to set limits on profits, some form of public intervention is necessary to assure reasonable prices. In most countries, the state operates such enterprises directly; in the U.S., government operation is not the typical pattern, though found in some regions. Instead, public agencies regulate price and service standards but leave ownership and management in private hands.

Other reasons. This list does not exhaust the theoretical bases for government activity, even where there is a general presumption in favor of doing things privately. The government has responsibility for general economic policy to *prevent depression and inflation*, matters discussed elsewhere in this book. The use of the *power of eminent domain*, under which the government can force people to give up land and to move, say, to permit a highway to be built or for slum clearance, may lead to government activity, because we do not entrust this power to private persons. Sometimes government activity is just a question of *convenience* and *low cost*; for instance, weather forecasting could be a private enterprise and some of it is. But it is handy to have one central data-collecting agency and to have it issue forecasts; it costs very little, and provides information to everybody.

A More Active Role for Government

Many Americans take a different philosophical position. Rather than limit government to situations in which the private market fails, they see government in three additional roles: (1) as a competing source of initiative; (2) as an influence on the pattern of private consumption; and (3) as a means of redistributing income.

Government as a source of initiative. Initiative and innovation can appear anywhere in a society. Managers in the public sector may see an opportunity to provide some service in a new or better way, just as in the private sector. Most government programs are quite far removed from commercial undertakings, and hence initiative is not likely to be applied competitively with private enterprises. But there are exceptions. The issue then arises whether the public agency that introduced the innovation should be allowed to develop it.

The Tennessee Valley Authority, which produces electric power (besides providing navigation, flood control, and other services) is an example of government initiative. In its heyday, the TVA had exceptional foresight in realizing

11

the potential of a high-volume, low-cost market for power; it also had the most efficient steam power plants in the world.[4]

Why? In the 1930s when TVA was organized, the private power industry was handicapped by the low profits and the negative psychology of the depression; the TVA, a major social experiment, attracted some of the finest young talent available. Today, private companies have the means of matching TVA's technical efficiency, and the huge size of the potential market for low-cost electricity at low rates is now appreciated by the entire power industry.

In America, with its many centers of private initiative, such examples of successful government enterprise are rare and usually associated with depression.[5] In contrast, in some less-developed countries, where the number of potential entrepreneurs is very small, one can expect government to play a sizable innovating role, even in industry.

Changing the pattern of consumption. In some situations, government rejects the decisions of consumers in the market and substitutes its own judgment. This is atypical in America, apart from discouraging the use of drugs, liquor, and tobacco through regulation and high taxes, and setting standards to protect consumers in such fields as packaging and auto safety. But there are cases where government acts to increase the supply and lower the cost of some goods or service, or even compels its consumption. Housing is the most substantial instance. The federal government has numerous programs in this field: public housing projects for low-income families, government loans and mortgage guarantees, and a tax system that gives favored treatment to home ownership.

Insurance against certain economic hazards is another consumer service prescribed through the political process. Social security is, essentially, a compulsory pension scheme to insure against poverty in old age or disability. Medicare extends compulsory insurance to the health field.

Redistributing income. Some government activities are intended to redistribute income. Programs such as social security, welfare, and unemployment insurance are designed to maintain incomes where earned income is inadequate. In addition, some public works are built and some lines of production are subsidized (for example, agriculture) to raise the income of a particular group. The federal government built a billion dollar project to make part of the Arkansas River navigable. It is hard to justify this project in terms of the national economic benefit to be gained from the boat traffic that will move on this river. But the project is in a poor region with little prospect of improvement without government help. Building the waterway raises the income in the area, the construc-

---

[4] TVA also had the advantage of very favorable tax treatment and of having access to low-interest public capital, as its critics justly charge. But this does not explain away its genuine achievements.

[5] The mortgage insurance program of the Federal Housing Administration is another example. Started in 1934 as an antidepression measure, this program has earned many millions in premiums, building up a large insurance reserve. But who could have the foresight at the bottom of the depression to see that the default rate on insured mortgages would be almost negligible while people would eagerly pay an insurance premium of ½ percent?

tion activity itself generates some local income, and the navigable river will improve the marketing of local crops and may attract industry. It might be cheaper to pay cash subsidies instead of authorizing a huge construction project, but subsidies would be politically unacceptable.

The Socialist Approach

Farther to the left on the political spectrum is the socialist approach to the scope of government: if other things are roughly equal, let an activity be public rather than private. Following Marxist doctrine that the private ownership of the means of production leads to the inevitable exploitation of the workers, industry should be owned by the workers acting through their government, and private ownership of capital becomes suspect. The most doctrinaire socialist would admit that government cannot run everything efficiently, that some things must be left to private enterprise. Even in Russia, a tiny sector of petty merchants and handicrafts survives, and farmers on collectives are allowed small plots of their own to cultivate; and in Yugoslavia, a less doctrinaire country, the state enterprises have some of the characteristics of private enterprises, with much independent decision making by the firms' managers, some price determination in markets, and wages and salaries tied to enterprise profits.

The problems of public finance in socialist countries differ in some important respects from those in a private enterprise economy. With industry state owned, the government must determine the economy's price and production policies. Production decisions are made through a central plan that sets the production targets for industries and their plants. Price policies become an important instrument of public finance. By allowing itself high markups on costs, the government can raise funds to finance its activities, including new investments. On the whole, socialist countries have not used their tax systems to promote income equality as much as we have. They defend their attitude on the grounds that with capital publicly owned, the income distribution produced by the economic system is satisfactory.

In our own country, there is increasing questioning of the ability of government to undertake its proper tasks adequately within the capitalist framework. It has been argued that the concentration of political power, particularly the political influence of the owners of capital and the managers of the private corporations, is so great that government is not able to take the necessary measures: it cannot provide the social services, the public outlays to assure minimum incomes, or take the regulatory steps to counteract the external diseconomies created by the productive process. For example, although it may be clear enough what prohibitions or taxes would suffice to neutralize the tendencies to pollute our waters or our atmosphere, the politico-economic system may be incapable of enacting the measures that are understood to be needed. Therefore, even if one accepts the view that the scope of government activity should be limited, other things equal, one might still come to the conclusion that a mixed system

13

inherently cannot work and that therefore the socialist alternative becomes a necessity.

The consideration of alternative economic systems is beyond the scope of this book.[6] But keep in mind that not all people share the philosophical point of view that favors private over public activity. In some of the less-developed countries, it is capitalism that is on trial, and activities are likely to be conducted privately only if private operation can be shown to be superior.

CONTROVERSIAL BORDER AREAS
BETWEEN PRIVATE AND PUBLIC SECTORS

Most people in America pretty much agree on the proper scope of government. We assume that a mixed private-public system can be made to work tolerably. We want ordinary productive activities privately owned and run, and private goods allocated through free markets. We also agree that government must provide collective goods and other goods and services not suitable for market processes.

Our differences are not about capitalism versus socialism as economic systems. They are about certain sectors of the economy in which private companies and public agencies compete for the privilege of development. We differ about the extent and power of government regulation. In terms of the economy as a whole, the areas under dispute are small; in terms of controversy, considerable. Here are some cases of turf that is under dispute.

Electric power. The federal government entered this business when it produced power as a by-product of dams built for flood control and navigation. Later, it built pure power dams if they were part of a river basin program that was designed to accomplish the other objectives. And in the Tennessee Valley, after the private systems had been bought out and the river had been fully developed, the TVA built steam-electric plants, a precedent the private-power companies considered ominous. At its peak in 1958, federal public power accounted for 17 percent of all power sold in this country, but it receded thereafter. For a while, it appeared that the old battles would be refought over atomic energy, but now it is viewed as just one more form of power equipment. Skirmishes continue here and there.

Insurance. Issues keep cropping up in this field. In the 1930s, social security was considered a government invasion of the private insurance field although, in the event, private pension plans were probably stimulated by the heightened interest in this type of saving for old age. In the early 1960s, medical insurance for the aged became the point of controversy. Insurance companies

[6] Another book in this Series is devoted to that subject. See Gregory Grossman, *Economic Systems.*

and the American Medical Association argued that voluntary private plans could do the job soon. Advocates of compulsory public insurance contended that medical costs of the aged had become too high for their low income, making illness another economic disaster against which the government ought to provide security. Now that the Medicare program has become part of the accepted institutions of this country, this controversy has faded. Now the ground has shifted to the proper extent of compulsory public health insurance for everybody.

Communications satellites. A clear indication of our preference for regulated capitalism over public ownership can be seen in the recent controversies about the management of the new worldwide communications satellite system. The development of the rockets required to launch the satellites was inevitably a public undertaking. On the other hand, civil radio communication has traditionally been a private industry. The obvious policy alternatives were to (1) have the federal government build and operate the system, or (2) assign the task to the American Telephone and Telegraph Company, which would be the biggest user, and which has the research know-how. These solutions proved unattractive; government operation would be a public invasion of a new industry; A. T. and T. control would strengthen its position in international communications. Instead, a new kind of institution was invented, a private corporation called *Comsat*, which is partly owned by the major communication companies, partly by the general public, with exceptionally stringent government regulations.

In the 1970s, the initial domestic system of communications satellites is being built. Once more, the choice is against public ownership. But by this time, the government has a greater concern to create a competitive situation, and so it is devising means to encourage several private companies to participate in this new technology.

Other cases. There are numerous other cases where policy must decide the public-private mix of activity in some detail. What should be the government's role in providing the needed expansion of outdoor recreation facilities? Should we emphasize national parks, or should we make it easier for private interests to assemble the land necessary for a recreation area, perhaps regulating the impact on the area's ecology and aesthetics? Should local government agencies be allowed to build commercial office buildings such as the enormous World Trade Center in New York, using their preferential tax position to gain advantage over private developers? Issues of this type arise continuously as rival public and private organizations compete for the privilege of conducting the nation's economic activities.

To resolve these questions, more than economics is involved. Economic analysis may show how close to our notion of a collective good a specific activity comes, how significant the divergency between private and social benefits and costs may be, or whether it will result in excessive monopoly power. But these considerations have to be weighed against the costs of the concentration of power in the hands of government and the imperfections of public operation.

15

THE BALLOT BOX
VERSUS THE MARKET PLACE

Decisions in government and in the private economy are reached quite differently. Supply and demand in markets determine spending and production decisions in the private sector. In the public sector, these decisions are made through the political process. Viewed as decision-making machinery, the major differences are these:

Government decisions involve an element of compulsion. An individual in an ordinary market is free to purchase or not purchase, but once the government has decided to supply some service, all individuals are compelled to share in paying for it through taxation. In the case of collective goods, this is inevitable. Because they cannot be withheld, they cannot be financed through voluntary market decisions. Therefore, if a majority of individuals (or rather their elected representatives) feels that a collective good is worth its cost to the community, it will vote to have the government provide it and to tax everyone to pay for it. An individual affirmative vote on an expenditure and a tax is not a decision to actually spend money; the spending and taxing will occur only if the majority approves, compelling everyone to share the cost. Thus, some people pay for services they do not want—even pacifists have to pay taxes for defense. Although this may be the only effective way of financing genuine collective goods, the same principle of compulsion applies to other kinds of public expenditures. Thus, all taxpayers contribute to the financing of agriculture, veterans' benefits, housing, and numerous other programs, even though many people may have no desire for them.[7]

Without the test of the market, there can be no assurance that a public service will actually render benefits greater than its cost. In the private sector, if a good does not provide satisfaction in excess of its cost, the company producing it will suffer losses; but governments collect their taxes even if a specific good that they supply proves unsatisfactory.

The political process is an insensitive choice mechanism. Government provides many services. But the voters can be expected to assess only a very small number of issues in any one election. Thus, the voter has to register his preference about a package of issues, whereas in the market place he can decide about each good separately.

Decisions made by the political process reflect the distribution of political power among pressure groups, regions, and the like. This influences the pattern of government expenditures. The groups that are well-organized receive more

16   [7] Not all expenditures are financed this way. A few, such as power projects, produce revenues sufficient to pay their cost. Others, such as highways, are paid for out of earmarked taxes levied on the users.

benefits than the rest and succeed in redistributing income from the unorganized to themselves. What is more, hardly any expenditure program, regardless of its importance to the country as a whole, is unaffected by the distribution of power. The location of space research facilities, the closing of defense installations, and other such decisions are influenced at least in a minor way by political strength. The pattern of distribution of public-works spending is more heavily determined by politics than by more rational criteria.

These considerations make the political process look inferior to the market mechanism. But there are some points on the other side.

In the market place, dollars are votes; in the political process, each person has one vote. A society in which all the voting was done by dollars would be inequitable. In a sense, the political process represents a safety valve for our capitalist system that modifies the income distribution produced in the market. This is clearly seen in such programs as public assistance and unemployment insurance, which aid individuals for whom the economic system is yielding particularly low incomes. But it is also illustrated by housing and agricultural programs, in which we reject the results of dollar voting in favor of spending decisions registered through the political process. With its different distribution of voting rights, the political process will produce a result different from that of the market. And after all, ours is a democracy of people, not of dollars.

In some situations, the market system cannot operate effectively. For true collective goods, there is no alternative to collective action, and these include such important matters as our personal security and the defense of our liberties. Even where goods are marketable, divergencies between private and social benefits and costs or the presence of monopoly power may cause markets to produce imperfect results.

The relevant comparison is not between perfect markets and imperfect governments, nor between faulty markets and all-knowing, rational, benevolent governments, but between inevitably imperfect institutions. The general recognition of the imperfection of all the alternatives may account for the decline of doctrinaire socialism or of doctrinaire laissez faire-ism in the United States. Perhaps it also accounts for the de facto stability in the division between the private and public sectors in our economy that has prevailed in the last two decades.

WHAT BALANCE BETWEEN PRIVATE AND PUBLIC SPENDING?

With the decision processes so different for private and public spending, how can there be an efficient division of spending—and hence of resource use—between private and public purposes? It is important that some reasonable balance be struck. An economy, no matter how efficiently it meets consumers' demands for private goods and services, will not be performing adequately if

17

public services are insufficient and of poor quality. What good is the most desirable of automobiles if the roads are congested, badly surfaced, and unsafe? What is the satisfaction of a home in the suburbs if the children go to crowded schools and are taught by teachers too harried to do their job?

A proper balance between private and public spending is, then, one of the performance criteria of an economic system, one of the key elements in judging the efficiency of resource allocation. Yet, there are a good many obstacles to the achievement of this goal. Professor Galbraith[8] has argued that our economic system imparts a systematic bias against public spending. The advertising industry and the product development divisions of our large corporations are fully devoted to the creation of new and more intense wants for private goods. Every magazine, billboard, and television program stimulates our desire to spend. Evidence of social imbalance abounds. Our investment in public beaches and parks is visibly inadequate for a rising population with increasing leisure time. Compare the physical state of your local hospital with your local department store: why should one be more attractive than the other?

In response to these concerns, the United States has sharply stepped up its efforts in some public fields. For example, federal expenditures for education rose from $400 million to $8.8 billion between 1957 and 1972, for health, from $500 million to $16 billion. If there was an imbalance between private and public spending, the redressing is coming at a rapid pace. Presidential leadership has proved to be a match for the advertising industry.

But the nagging question remains whether increased outlays will remove the anomalies that caught the public's eye. Will increased spending assure every child of a minimum quality education? Will the rapid advances in medical science reach towns large and small, people rich and poor? The answers to these questions depend upon the government's ability to use its resources effectively. The next chapter deals with that theme.

SUMMARY

Government plays a large role in the economy, as regulator of the private sector, as supplier of public services, and in many other ways. Public finance is the study of government's taxing and spending activities.

Government absorbs one-fifth of the total output of the nation's goods and services. It also redistributes large amounts of income through a system of transfer payments to households, to businesses, and from one level of government to another. Government expenditures have been rising over a long period, both absolutely and relative to total output. In recent years, the greatest growth has been at the state and local levels.

The definition of the proper scope of government activities can be partly

[8] J. K. Galbraith is responsible for the modern formulation of this issue in his famous book, *The Affluent Society* (New York: Houghton Mifflin, 1958).

based on such theoretical concepts as collective goods, differences in private and social benefits and costs, and natural monopolies. But these must be combined with philosophical values about the relative desirability of public and private action. The United States has generally favored private over public action, but not all countries share our preference in this matter.

Decisions in the private sector are made through the market mechanism, in the public sector through the political process. Each of these processes has its own advantages and imperfections. The market is free of compulsion and permits more sensitive expression of individual preferences. But its votes are based on dollars, and individuals are not equals in their possession of these voting rights. The political process is based on individual votes. The redistributions of income that the government carries out are a safety valve of our capitalist system.

The frontier between the private and the public sectors has been stabilized in the last two decades, after some extension of the public sector under the New Deal. There is a wide consensus in the U.S. today to support the present line. A few fields remain in dispute and are subject to much controversy, but these represent a very small share of economic activity.

The proper balance between public and private spending is one of the key performance criteria of an economic system. In recent years, the United States has reexamined this question, and stepped up its efforts in some public areas substantially.

Efficiency

in Government Expenditures

CHAPTER TWO

A fifth of the nation's output is allocated, not by individual choices in markets, but by public decision making. Can economic principles be derived to guide these decisions so that resource allocation in the public sector will be efficient, so that the resources will be employed to reach public objectives effectively and without waste? In this chapter, we study two problems: (1) How are decisions actually made in the public sector? and (2) How can technical economic analysis contribute to the process?

BUDGETING

Although it is the general political process that determines government expenditures, it is through budgeting that the specific decisions are reached. A budget is a detailed statement of a government's expected expenditures and revenues. The executive branch of government reaches it expenditure and tax decisions in the preparation of this document; the legislative branch considers the proposals and votes the fiscal plans of the government into law.

The federal budget covers a fiscal year, running from July 1 to the following June 30. But the decision making process starts more than a year earlier, when agencies prepare their preliminary program proposals. These are reviewed in the light of presidential guidelines on total spending. Detailed budget requests are then made by the agencies in the fall, and from October to December, the president, working with his elite Office of Management and Budget, reviews and pares down the agency requests, which typically outrun what he wishes to spend. By weighing the urgency of the programs against the fiscal needs of the economy as a whole, he decides on an overall spending policy. He has to decide whether to balance the budget or to run a surplus or a deficit, and then to bring agency requests into line with his overall fiscal goals.

Early in January, the president sends his budget to Congress. In a growing number of cases, the spending proposals are first considered by the oversight committee concerned with each program, such as the Foreign Relations and Military Affairs Committees, and then reviewed by the houses of Congress. When new legislation is needed, the oversight committee must act before funds can be voted. They vote *authorizations* for programs and specify policies governing them. But this is only the first stage; the Appropriations Committees and the House and Senate still have to vote the *appropriations* of money. Frequently, less is appropriated than is authorized because the Appropriation Committees tend to be stingier with the public's money than the committees devoted to specific programs.

The appropriations give the president the right to make contracts and to spend the money, and usually, but not always, after some further passage of time, the appropriation leads to an *expenditure*—that is, to the actual disbursal of money. In some of the largest fields, including defense and space, the delay between appropriation and expenditure is so long and the backlogs of unexpended appropriations so large that Congress feels it has lost control over the expenditures.

Although the period of decision-making appears very long for a fast-moving world, the plans can be and are changed all along the way. Many key decisions by the president are postponed to the last possible moment in December. If economic or international conditions change during the spring, he can change his requests. Congress also watches developments as it acts on the budget and reacts to them. Even during the fiscal year itself, the president can decide not to spend all the money voted or go back to Congress for supplementary appropriations.

Before 1920, the United States had no integrated budget at all. Appropriations requests of individual agencies were considered strictly piecemeal, and if a congressman, a newspaper reporter, or just plain voter wished to discover the government's total spending plans, he would have found it virtually impossible to do so. With government very much smaller then, there was less need for a comprehensive view and for weighing expenditure requests against one another. The heavy expenditures during World War I which produced a deficit much larger than planned, plainly indicated the need for a budget. President Taft had advocated the use of a budget earlier, but the Congress refused to approve its adoption.

We have come a long way since then. Today, the budget is an informative document, showing how the departments and their agencies spend their money. To find out what the federal government does, take a look at *The Budget of the*

21

United States Government.[1] The president's submission of the budget to the Congress each January enables the entire nation to take a look at government activities.

The unity of the budget disappears once it reaches the Congress, as separate committees and separate subcommittees of the Appropriation Committees take up the various parts. It has repeatedly been recommended that there be a congressional committee to take up the entire budget each year, to bring all expenditures decisions together, and to deal with such general issues of fiscal policy as budget levels and surpluses or deficits. This is a rather utopian proposal. Congress has to be concerned with the detailed decisions. It does not decide to raise or lower the budget as a whole, but works through the specific items. No one committee could deal with all the questions at once. Under the present setup, however, it is important that the congressmen voting on specific expenditure requests have the overall economic and financial situation in mind. The budget makes it possible for them to do so.

BENEFIT-COST ANALYSIS

Can economic analysis be applied to budget decisions? The remainder of this chapter explores some of the possibilities.

The ideal principle for budget decisions is clear enough. *Push expenditures for each public purpose to that point where the benefit of the last dollar spent is greater than the dollar of cost.* The line *MB* in Fig. 2–1 shows how the benefit resulting from additional expenditures on project *A* first rises, then falls as more is spent. Some moderate level of expenditures for, say, highways, yields very great benefits because this money can be spent on breaking the worst bottlenecks, reducing deaths, injuries, property damage, time spent traveling, gasoline consumption, and wear and tear on car and driver. Greater expenditures may

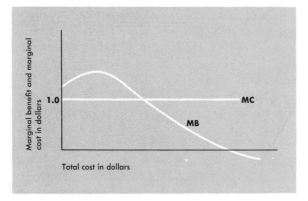

FIG. 2–1 Equating marginal benefits and costs. Because quantity is measured by dollars spent, the marginal cost curve is just a line parallel to the base, equal to 1.0 (the marginal cost of an extra dollar of spending is a dollar).

[1] *The Budget of the United States Government.* Superintendent of Documents, Washington, D.C. 20402 ($2.50).

still yield benefits greater than cost, but there is a point where the additional projects undertaken are in more remote, less traveled places, raising road quality beyond the level for which the cost can be justified by the additional benefits. Thus, frequently, there comes into play a *law of diminishing benefit*, similar to the laws of diminishing returns and diminishing rates of substitution for private goods.[2]

Equating marginal benefits and costs, if it could be done, would solve two problems of resource allocation. It would assure that every expenditure yields a benefit at least equal to the value of goods foregone in the private sector. It would also assure that an expenditure does not prevent a more valuable public expenditure in some other field. Thus, the principle assures that benefits of marginal expenditures exceed opportunity costs both in the private and the public sectors.

An Example: Design of a Flood Control Project

Flood control is one field of expenditures to which the government applies analysis of benefits and costs. Table 2–1 provides an illustration that is simplified, but typical of actual cases. It shows flood damage without protection in a typical year and the lowered damage figures that result from progressively more ambitious flood protection plans.

Plan *C*, the medium-sized reservoir, is the best plan. Although it costs $8,000 more than the smaller reservoir, it averts an additional $9,000 of damages, so the marginal benefits exceed the marginal costs. A further increment, going to the larger reservoir, would cost an extra $12,000 yet yield only $7,000

Table 2–1 BENEFIT-COST ANALYSIS OF FLOOD CONTROL FOR BRINK VALLEY

Plan	Annual Cost of Project	Average Annual Damage	Benefit (Reduction of Damage)
Without protection	0	$38,000	0
Plan A—levees	$ 3,000	32,000	$ 6,000
Plan B—small reservoir	10,000	22,000	16,000
Plan C—medium reservoir	18,000	13,000	25,000
Plan D—large reservoir	30,000	6.000	32,000

Plan	Marginal Benefit	Marginal Cost
No plan	0	0
Plan A	$ 6,000	$ 3,000
Plan B	10,000	7,000
Plan C	9,000	8,000
Plan D	7,000	12,000

[2] But not always! Sometimes, as in curing depressed areas or in urban renewal, only a large-scale effort may succeed. It may be better to pour large sums into a few places than to spread funds thinly among many.

of benefits. Thus, this marginal outlay fails the test of having benefits exceed costs—that is, marginal benefits are less than marginal costs.

The example shows that the principle of equating benefits and costs at the margin can be applied to some public expenditures. But a number of qualifications must be kept in mind:

1. Real-world data are always subject to error. Actual damages will differ from the projections. The frequency of floods cannot be predicted precisely, nor can their damages, particularly for rare but large floods. (Who knows what damage the biggest flood in a thousand years would do? Our history goes back only 360 years, and the early settlers did not spend their time collecting statistics.) Engineering and economic uncertainties must be reckoned with. Construction frequently proves to be more complicated and more costly than expected; prices applied to value benefits may change unpredictably.

2. The definition of *benefit* does not distinguish to whom the benefits or costs accrue, yet this is usually of concern in public undertakings.

3. Most important, it must be possible to measure economic benefits in dollars and cents. Even in the field of flood control—a rather simple one for economic analysis—the definition of *benefit* is ambiguous. To what extent is lost production made up elsewhere later on? What is the loss attributable to the feeling of insecurity caused by floods, not to mention that most intractable valuation problem: the worth of a saved human life?

Another Example: Benefits and Costs of Drop-Out Prevention

The "War on Poverty" has led to a great increase in federal programs of investment in human resources, in health, education, and training. If there is to be assurance that these efforts will be fruitful, there must be economic study of the benefits and costs. Such analysis is only in its infancy, indeed is one of the most exciting frontiers of economic science. The following example is adapted from a pioneer work of Professor Burton Weisbrod of the University of Wisconsin, who analyzed a small program to reduce the drop-out rate in a St. Louis High School. His conclusions were rather negative, and may be peculiar to the particular case. But the method is more generally applicable, and it produced some startling insights even in this very limited application.

In this project, a group of over 400 potential drop-outs was selected. Half were given extra counseling and special help in finding and retaining part-time jobs. The other half received only the normal school services. They served as a control group, to see what difference the special efforts to prevent teen-agers from dropping out of high school would make.

The main benefit of such a project is the increased income earned because high school is completed. The average high school graduate could be expected to earn $2,750 more than a drop-out in the particular community, over his lifetime.[3] He would have better jobs and suffer fewer and shorter spells of unemployment. The income gain associated with completing high school is twice as high for whites as for nonwhites, and a third greater for girls than for boys. White girls would expect an extra $4,600 of income, Negro boys only $1,750. No wonder the drop-out rate was especially high for Negro boys.

Despite the intensive counseling, 44 percent of the group receiving help quit school before graduation. In the control group, 52 percent dropped out, so an average improvement of 8 percent could be credited to the special program of drop-out prevention. Given an income benefit of $2,750 for a prevented drop-out, and a reduction in the probability of a counseled student dropping out of 8 percent, the average benefit per counseled student would be $220.

The costs in this project were large. Perhaps partly because it was an experiment, it cost a total of $520 to help each student, so, in a narrow sense, cost exceeded benefit. But, of course, this comparison is not a complete one. It makes no allowance for the human benefits of equipping youths to earn their own way rather than to drift from unemployment insurance to public assistance, possibly from delinquency to jail. Nor does it allow a benefit for breaking the circles of poverty that trap families from generation to generation. Nevertheless, the experiment did raise these questions: Does counseling to prevent drop-outs come too late? After all, the benefit of the project was kept low by the failure to prevent more drop-outs (though preventing 8 drop-outs out of 52—or 1 out of 7—is quite a bit in human terms!). If we want to equip all our youths with the high school education necessary in the modern job world, we apparently should give extra help to the disadvantaged long before they are drop-out candidates. Another implication is the necessity to provide good job opportunities that will utilize the education. Dropping out of school is an economic decision, in which the individual weighs gains and costs. The drop-out rates were highest for those who could expect least from finishing school.

Uses of Benefit-Cost Analysis

Can the benefit-cost principle, then, serve to determine the proper allocation of resources for public expenditures? If it could, the problem of the optimal balance between public and private spending would yield to economic analysis. And as we saw in the preceding chapter, it is a most fundamental problem of resource allocation in a mixed economy. But unfortunately, the dollar yardstick cannot be adequately applied to the benefits of many of the fields of government activity. The benefits of defense, space research, foreign aid, police protection, or the administration of justice cannot be readily expressed in dollar terms. Education, housing, and highways, which are believed to provide considerable monetary benefits, so far have not yielded to reliable measurement. Their benefit

---

[3] This figure is based on an interest rate of 5 percent to compute the present value of future income gains.

is widely diffused and partly noneconomic. Could a democracy survive without an educated citizenry? What is the net gain from clearing a slum? Thus the benefit-cost principle can be applied only in limited cases like flood control, electric power production, the Post Office, some transportation and recreation facilities—mostly in fields where benefits are primarily economic, tangible, and measurable.

Nonetheless, the benefit-cost principle is of great importance. At the very least, it is a useful antidote to two approaches that are widely employed and that are pretty sure to lead to poor results. The first of these is the *requirements approach*. It says that a country "needs" X thousand more new housing units, W million gallons of water, Y dozen nuclear submarines, Z thousand more classrooms by 1980, and that this need is so clear that it must be fulfilled regardless of the cost. In fact, there is always some cost that the "requirement" is not worth. And adding up the "requirements" as seen by the proponents of each program always yields fantastically expensive results. Economic resources are scarce; tough choices have to be made between competing programs, and strongly voiced assertions about requirements and needs do not really help us to reach wise decisions. Benefits must be balanced against costs at the margin.

The other fallacious approach is the *what can we afford* or *budget first* approach. It determines the total to be spent before looking at the benefits. Although usually employed by opponents of spending who suggest that an extra dollar beyond the arbitrarily set amount would somehow bankrupt the country, the approach also has a spender's variant: "Why are we spending only X percent of our GNP on—fill in your favorite government service—when we spend Y percent on liquor and tobacco?"

A firm grasp of the benefit-cost principle will not provide easy answers to expenditure choices. Instead, it forces us to pass judgment on the worth of the expenditure at issue, to see if it is worth its tax cost, and whether it represents the best use of the public money. It also focuses the attention of decision makers on the margins, where the decisions are made. It does not ask: "Is defense worth its cost?" but rather, "Would an extra billion of defense yield an important enough improvement in our strength to be worth the cost?" This is the sort of inescapable question that the president and Congress have to face every year, and that they have to answer even where precise measurement of benefit is impossible.

THE PRICING
OF PUBLIC SERVICES

Pricing can be used to improve resource use in the public sector. For that limited range of public services that are marketable, the government can achieve equality of marginal benefit and marginal cost. It has the choice of providing them free or charging for them. The absence of a charge makes for maximum use, but it also leads to waste.

Pricing is largely a question of economic efficiency. We know from price theory that a market economy requires prices as signaling devices to indicate to producers what value consumers place on their outputs, and conversely, to indicate to consumers what the costs of providing goods and services are to the economy. In the private sector, the rule for pricing is this: *Price, in an efficient economy, is equal to the cost of supplying the marginal unit of service, that is, equal to marginal cost.* With consumers adjusting to market prices, they will purchase goods in such quantities that the marginal rates of substitution (or ratios of marginal utilities) among the various commodities will equal their relative prices.

In principle, this rule could be carried over to many government services; but in practice, governments frequently underprice their services, sometimes because of the influence of pressure groups, sometimes as a matter of philosophy. When goods are underpriced, purchasers will undervalue them and use them wastefully. Here are a few examples:

Postal service. The postal service runs at a large loss because postal rates are kept low. The result is just what one would expect. Being cheap, the postal service is used wastefully, as the astronomical volume of junk advertising mail attests. This is one of the causes of the deficit. Magazines and books enjoy low rates and add their bit to the losses. In addition, the low rates and the grudging financing of the deficits by Congress have kept the postal service poor, too poor to be able to finance a proper modernization program. Contrast the post offices with the telephone companies, privately operated enterprises in a similar business, that have a more rational rate structure and that are able to conduct research and take full advantage of technological progress.

National parks. The pricing of the use of national parks has been a matter of philosophy. The National Park Service has preferred to keep the parks either free or available at very low charges to assure maximum use. If one assumes that the marginal cost of additional use of a national park is very low, this policy makes sense. But it is now clear that as use goes up, additional facilities have to be provided. Conversely, as the facilities are improved, more people are eager to use the parks. For these reasons, the Park Service has raised some of its charges and has discovered in the process that users do value the parks highly and are generally willing to pay the higher prices cheerfully. It now looks as if higher prices will lead to better parks and greater use.

Roads. The pricing of roads is a particularly complicated but important case. Traditionally, the U.S. has provided roads without charge, except for tolls on some bridges and some state turnpikes. An obviously inefficient allocation of resources has resulted from this policy. This is seen most clearly in the case of congested city streets. No charge is made at the time of use. As taxpayers, the motorists pay for the city streets, but their tax bill is not related to the fre- **27** quency of use. Thus, in day-to-day decision making, the motorist considers the city streets free. More and more commuters use private automobiles rather than public transit facilities. The resultant congestion leads to demands for heavy expenditures to improve the roads. This is a losing battle because the additional roads, again provided free to the motorist, divert more traffic from mass transit systems to private cars, producing further congestion and the need for more roads. Economists have long advocated that the commuter motorist pay the marginal cost he imposes on society, the cost of roads plus his contribution to congestion. If he had to pay a substantial toll, the market test thus provided would indicate whether the pleasure of driving his own car into town was worth the social cost. Access roads might have toll stations, street permits could be issued, or parking could be made expensive.[4] But the practical men of the world have ruled out this solution, and so we can look forward to an endless cycle of congested highways, new construction at great cost, more motorists, more congestion.

INSTITUTIONALIZING THE USE OF ECONOMIC PRINCIPLES: THE PPBS SYSTEM

Attempting to apply economic principles more fully to the public sector, the federal government developed an elaborate set of procedures in the 1960s, called the *Program Planning and Budgeting System.* Principles developed in the Department of Defense for evaluating weapons systems were applied to civilian expenditures. Marginal costs and benefits are estimated, and only those projects that can pass the economic tests are to be undertaken. But principles are not enough. In the private sector, it is the market process that assures the application of economic criteria. In the public sector, an institutional process must be set up that assures that the economic principles are actually applied and receive a hearing in the political decision making. The following steps would help assure this result.

First, the organizational structure should be arranged in such a way that one decision unit is responsible for a given objective. In that way, one authority is confronted with a choice among all the alternatives that can be used to achieve that objective and can rationally seek out the best one. For example, Polaris submarines and Minuteman missiles are alternative means for achieving strategic objectives. If key budget decisions are made within the Navy and within the Air Force, then Polaris competes with other ships and Minuteman missiles with airplanes, rather than having the two missile systems competing with each other. By concentrating this choice process in the hands of the Secretary of Defense, the possibility was created of systematically searching for the most effective, least-cost missile system.

[4] Gasoline taxes do not provide a test because gasoline use does not correspond to the social costs of being on the highways during the peak periods.

In contrast, the development of the nation's water resources is in the hands of competing agencies in different departments, the Army Corps of Engineers in the Defense Department, the Bureau of Reclamation of the Department of the Interior, and other agencies. In the absence of one unified center of decision making, there is no assurance that the best development is pursued on each river, as each agency promotes its particular purposes. A Department of Natural Resources can be expected to assure more rational development. The desire of recent presidents to combine cabinet departments to more closely match our national objectives reflects their wish to allow choices to be made more rationally.

Second, costs must be viewed over a number of years. For most new programs, the first-year cost is small, and all too frequently that is all that will be found in the budget. If decision making is to be rational, the total cost over the entire program life has to be considered, not just the initial year's expense. Under the PPBS system, programs are costed for five years.

Third, decision making is improved by creating an institutional setup under which the pressures on the decision makers lead them in the direction of economic choices. In the private market economy, self-interest and the discipline of the profit-and-loss statement serve to produce rational production decisions. In the public sector, decision makers do not maximize profits. Instead, they operate by the criteria that are imposed on them by the organization in which they operate. If the criteria are designed to promote the achievement of the public-policy objectives, a process not very different from the market mechanism will occur; if the criteria are badly designed, waste and failure will ensue. For example, military supply officers maintain inventories of clothing, ammunition, equipment, and the like. A "good" supply officer has the things his men need; a "bad" one is always running out of things. Inevitably, supply officers become hoarders, eager to obtain as many supplies as they can to be ready for all contingencies. Under modern conditions, where weapons become obsolete rapidly, this hoarding produces waste. Inventories become too big, tie up capital, and many items become obsolete before they are used. A proper criterion for supply decisions takes account both of the losses suffered when an item is unavailable and the costs of stocking it. In recent years, the armed services have adopted such economic criteria, and supply officers are now judged not only by their skill in obtaining large inventories but also by their ability to keep the total costs down.

Incentive Contracts
for Government Procurement

With the Defense Department spending over $20 billion a year for equipment, efficiency in procurement is particularly important. The government usually grants contracts to manufacturers to supply specific items. Where the item is standard and requires little technological novelty—such as uniforms, gasoline, tires, and food—contracts are let by competitive bidding after public notice. This assures a competitive result through the normal processes of the

29

private economy. A large part of procurement, however, is for complicated equipment (missiles and the like), frequently of a type that has never been manufactured before, and sometimes still requiring development. Here, competitive bidding is impossible because the product cannot be specified precisely nor can there be assurance that the manufacturer will in fact succeed in producing it. In the past, a "cost-plus" contract was used, under which the manufacturers produced the item and the government agreed to pay whatever the cost turned out to be plus a fixed percentage for profit or a fixed fee. This system provides no incentive for the manufacturer to keep costs down; in fact, the higher the cost, the higher his profit. This is really backward economics! An alternative would be to offer the manufacturer a contract that specifies a fixed price, leaving any cost-saving wholly as extra profit. This, after all, is the incentive that reduces costs in the private economy. But this approach is not feasible where the costs are as unknown as they are in advanced technology, for the government would have to offer private companies a very high price to make it worthwhile for them to run the large risks that the fixed-price contract would entail.[5] It is not uncommon for weapons systems to cost more than twice as much as originally expected. Nor is there any assurance that technical specifications can be met at any price.

To steer a middle path between removing all incentives for cost cutting and having to pay very high risk premiums, the government has experimented with incentive contracts, under which the manufacturer keeps a fraction of any cost-saving below the original estimate, and is penalized by a fraction of any excesses of costs above the estimates. Such contracts are no substitute for the normal workings of competition, but at least they introduce some incentives to keep costs down rather than to inflate them. On-time delivery and technical quality have also been promoted by incentive contracts.

CONCLUDING NOTE:
THE POLITICAL REALITY

The application of economics to public expenditures is still in its infancy, and it would be rash indeed to evaluate the present decision processes in terms of the ideals of economic theory. But here are a few observations on the actual process.

1. Present decisions rely heavily on the activities of pressure groups at several stages of the budget cycle both in the executive branch and the Congress. Lobbying is a highly organized activity in this country, and many public needs

---

[5] The government experimented with this approach in developing the C5A, the large transport plane. The Lockheed Corporation won the fixed price contract and went virtually bankrupt when technology proved tougher to develop and costs generally inflated. At the last moment, the government relented and agreed to pay a few hundred million dollars of cost-overruns.

are brought to public attention by this process. But programs that would help the unorganized are likely to be too small. The social imbalance among categories of public spending is probably as great as or greater than the imbalance between private and public spending.

2. An old program is a good program. Once it has existed for a period, a program generates its own clientele, both inside and outside the government, that has a vested interest in its continuance. It is virtually impossible to discontinue a program. With total spending possibilities always outrunning likely revenues, new programs encounter difficult sledding.

3. Our political system gives more groups the power to exercise vetoes than to initiate new programs. For a program to get started, it must not only have the positive backing of lots of people, but it must encounter relatively few vetoes.

4. Bargaining is an important part of decision making. There is bargaining between rival government agencies, between the Office of Management and Budget and the operating agencies, between the president and the congressional committees, and among representatives of different regions and other groups within the Congress. The viewpoints of interested parties are also expressed through congressional hearings and informal lobbying. This process of bargaining is untidy and follows no simple, logical principles. But it does usually guarantee that important issues are not overlooked. It cuts down the kind of gross mistakes that the more efficient decision processes of totalitarian governments will occasionally produce.

SUMMARY

Expenditure decisions in the public sector are reached through the budgeting process. A budget contains the planned expenditures and revenues for a fiscal year. The federal government follows a highly sophisticated budgeting process, in which the detailed requests of spending agencies are weighed against the needs of overall fiscal policy.

Economic principles can be applied to budgeting to improve the efficiency of resource allocation in the public sector. The principle that marginal benefit must exceed marginal cost can be applied in some limited fields. But for a large part of government expenditures, no objective measure of benefit can be defined. Economic pricing of marketable public services can help to assure an efficient use of resources.

To achieve rational choices, the decision making process must be properly designed. Relevant alternatives for accomplishing each objective must be weighed against one another. Expenditures must be clearly identified with the objectives they are to accomplish. The pressures on decision makers must be of the sort that will lead to the application of proper criteria. And costs over the entire period of a program, not just for a year, have to be taken into account.

The Public Finances

of State and Local Governments

CHAPTER THREE

Chapter One wrestled with the question: What activities should be carried out publicly rather than privately? Once the scope of public activity is defined, it remains to decide on the proper division of activity among the several levels of government in our federal system —what should be done by the federal government, what by state and local governments.

In some New England towns, the open town meeting, with every citizen eligible to vote, is still the prevailing legislature. Here is pure democracy. When it comes to public finance, the residents of the town register their own judgments about the benefits and cost of expenditures. The town officials may submit their budget, but the town meeting usually has ideas of its own that keep the government efficient and the cost low.

When you contrast this decision-making process with Washington or the state capitals—where legislators deal with a wide range of issues, many of them remote from their own experience, pressured by lobbyists seeking benefits without costs for their group, and impose uniform policies on a wide range of communities of different circumstances and desires—you see the advantage of having a federal system in which vigorous local governments handle what problems they can.

One of the most intriguing problems of the economics of public finance is to determine the level of government most appropriate for handling each of the public services. This chapter deals with that question as well as the general financial problems of state and local governments and examines some possible solutions.

32

THE ADVANTAGES
OF LOCAL GOVERNMENT

Many people feel that whatever can be done privately, should be. If it must be done by government, let it be at the local level, or as a second choice, by the states. This view is based on the belief that the total power of government should be kept as restricted as possible to protect the individual and private institutions, and that power should remain diffused rather than centralized. Furthermore, only the exercise of governmental functions keeps local governments healthy, and it is they that provide the main opportunity for individual participation in government. Washington is far removed from the daily lives of most of us. We vote for presidents and congressmen, but that is very different from voting in a New England town meeting, or serving on a school board, or running for local alderman. These are political arguments, but they have their economic counterparts.

1. Expenditure decisions may be made more rationally in a small government than in a big one because of the greater coincidence between the distribution of the benefits and costs. In the case of a proposed new federal program, individuals—and their congressmen—take less cognizance of the resultant increase in taxes because the share that they or their district will have to pay will be small. In local government, the resultant tax cost usually can be seen more immediately by the taxpayers. Even in local government, collective choices made through the political process are not subject to the market test. But when decisions are made for a small community, other things being equal, the rational market result is more likely to be approximated because judgment is apt to be better informed and the possibilities of making nonbeneficiaries pay are smaller.

2. A multiplicity of separate communities creates the possibility of some individual choice even about collective goods. You recall from Chapter One that one of the characteristics of a collective good was that all the members of the community had to enjoy the same level of the good regardless of their individual desires simply because it was supplied jointly to all of them. But where there are alternative communities, a new kind of choice is introduced. Each individual can elect to become a member of that community that offers him the combination of collective goods that he prefers. For example, in the typical metropolitan area with its core city and its numerous suburbs, one man may prefer to have his family live in a community that has excellent schools but high taxes; another, perhaps the head of a childless family or with children beyond school age, may prefer a poor school system and low taxes. Now, because a person can live in only one place, he cannot pick the precise combination of public services he prefers, but at least he has some choice about their general pattern. This process

33

of community selection tends to produce a greater coincidence of benefits and costs in public services. Typically, families who have a stake in education flock together in the suburbs, as do older couples or families who prefer not to send their children to public schools. Each receives the school system that he wants and is willing to pay for.

3. Decentralizing public functions at the state and local level permits each region to apply its own values to government programs. Unlike some of the smaller and more homogenous countries of Europe, the people in different parts of the United States have quite different ideas about the proper public responsibility in such fields as public assistance and unemployment benefits, about the nature of education, and even about the proper division between the private and the public sectors. Whatever government services are supplied at the state and local level can be provided in accordance with regional preferences; the national government must impose uniform standards if it is to undertake a program.

4. Decentralization also permits experimentation and pioneering by a few communities, which later on may set the standards for the rest of the country. Compare the American educational system with centralized systems in Western Europe and Japan. Here, the federal government has virtually no voice; state education departments are powerful in determining the curricula and setting standards in some parts of the country, while elsewhere the decision-making power is retained by the local school board. As a result, some schools are superlative, developing new teaching techniques, changing curricula with the needs of the times, and employing well-paid, highly qualified teachers. Other school systems vary from very good to downright poor, depending on the attitudes and the economic resources of the communities and states. In a country such as France, power is concentrated in the Ministry of Education, which determines curricula, picks textbooks, trains and hires teachers, even sets nationwide examitions for the students. The result is a greater uniformity among school systems, with less innovation and few schools of true excellence, but with fairly good schools even if the community is poor and does not value education highly.

5. The political process imposes regional spending patterns that reflect the distribution of political power. Whatever the national objectives of a federal program may be, there will be strong pressures to allocate funds in a regional pattern that reflects the political strength of different regions in the Congress. Expenditures at the local level also go through some similar log-rolling, but the possibilities may be more limited.

THE ADVANTAGES
OF NATIONAL PROGRAMS

The United States was originally established because of the need for a national government. Looked at from the limited perspective of economics, here are some of the factors requiring national action:

1. Certain public services are collective for the country as a whole, in the sense that they are provided jointly for all the individuals of the nation. Defense and other programs in support of our foreign policy are clearly of this character. Other public services are collective to a smaller community and thus can be provided through a government instituted for the smaller group. Police and fire protection are examples.

2. Some public services involve the national interest only to a degree, and reasonable men can differ over whether the national interest is sufficient to justify national programs. For example, the entire society has a stake in the education of its citizens. We all share the same political process, the quality of which depends on an educated citizenry. The cultural richness of our society as well as our effectiveness in accomplishing such tasks as the space effort and defense depend on the quality of our education. We all enjoy higher incomes because our labor force has a high average degree of education. And the national effort to reduce poverty is mainly an investment in the education and training of the poor. Are these factors sufficient to make education a national concern? Only to a limited extent. National programs are still largely confined to financial support of science in the schools and of higher education, and special grant programs for schools with poor children.

3. The superiority of the financial resources of the federal government tends to cause programs to gravitate to the national level. The federal government has appropriated some of the best revenue sources, particularly income taxation, and this has made it difficult for the state and local governments to find adequate funds. Competition among states for new industry has also limited the use of some taxes, especially taxes on business. Furthermore, average incomes are much higher in some states than in others. If a minimum level of a public service is to be assured everywhere, the wealthier states must help out the poorer states, as they do when the federal tax system is used for financing.

4. The willingness to undertake public services is sometimes greater at the national than at the state and local level. (Not everybody would consider this a virtue.) Although the same individuals elect officials at the several levels of government, the political choices that are made on spending matters will not necessarily be the same. Locally, heavily taxed property owners who are not likely to be sympathetic to spending may be particularly influential. The poor may have little power. Also, our most important media of mass communication are national, and hence it is easier to arouse popular interest in a problem or an objective on a nationwide rather than a local basis. Our attention is focused on Washington, not on our state capitals or on our cities and towns.

5. Finally, many state and local governments lack initiative and are just plain inefficient. They find it difficult to attract top quality personnel with the salaries they offer. In some areas, corruption is a serious problem. Even though many of the economic challenges to government in the present decade are at the state and local level—in such fields as education, urban renewal, and resource

35

development—the leadership necessary to formulate effective programs is all too often found only on the national scene.

POSTWAR FINANCES OF STATE
AND LOCAL GOVERNMENTS

We have already seen in Chapter One that the total expenditures of state and local governments have increased enormously in the postwar period. Outlays were $22.3 billion in 1950, but by 1971 they had reached $135 billion. No one would have predicted that state and local governments would prove capable of financing such enormous outlays, given the relatively low automatic response of their taxes to income growth. Such increases would have struck most experts as impossible; and in fact, a general financial crisis for state and local governments has been predicted repeatedly. Yet, in most areas, the revenue requirements have been met; Table 3–1 summarizes how it was accomplished.

The property tax, which had long been assumed not to respond to economic growth, yielded more than three times as much as it had 15 years earlier because of the growth of the tax base associated with the postwar building boom, higher rates, and improved administration. It had always been difficult to administer the tax, particularly in periods of inflation, when thoroughly unpopular reassessment of property values is necessary in order for the tax to keep pace with the price level. Nevertheless, in the face of the acute financial need, many communities did reassess to increase the size of the base and also increased the rates steadily.

Revenues from sales taxes increased sharply, partly in response to economic growth and higher rates, partly due to the adoption of general sales taxes

Table 3–1 REVENUES OF STATE AND LOCAL GOVERNMENTS
1950, 1971 (billions of dollars)

	1950	1971	Percentage Increase
Revenues			
Total	21.1	151.8	619
Property taxes	7.4	41.3	458
Sales and excise taxes	4.8	31.3	552
Personal income taxes	.8	12.7	1488
Corporation income taxes	.8	4.2	425
Contributions for social insurance	1.0	9.4	840
Other taxes	1.7	10.6	524
Motor vehicle licenses	.9	1.6	78
Other revenues from own sources	3.1	11.4	268
Grants-in-aid from federal government	2.3	29.3	1174

Source: National Income and Product Accounts, U.S. Department of Commerce.

in many states. Personal income taxes rose considerably, as more and more states and some cities adopted them. Corporation income taxes remained at low levels, as states found it difficult to tax national corporations for fear of losing their plants.

Grant-in-aid programs from the federal government also helped in a major way, rising from $2.3 to $29.6 billion. The federal government took over the financing of much of the highway program, increased its contribution to state and local welfare programs, and provided large new grant programs for education and health.

In the last decade, the demands on local finances rose very sharply. The cities became the focal point of our social problems as the poor were pushed off the land by industrialization. Unionization of public employees raised payroll costs. Congestion and pollution required major investments in local roads, sewers, and waste-treatment plants.

The inflation of the late 1960s and early 1970s also worsened the local public finances. Costs rose faster than the average because it is difficult to raise productivity in local services. Some revenues, such as income and sales taxes, respond to inflation; but others, such as property and excise taxes, do not respond automatically. When tight money made it impossible for many communities to borrow and the recession of 1970 slashed revenue growth, local governments fell into their worst financial situation since the Great Depression.

SOLUTIONS TO THE PROBLEMS
OF STATE AND LOCAL FINANCE

Because of the continued large increases in fiscal needs in the face of weakly financed resources, the search for new solutions has intensified.

The financial problem also differs among the states. Economic resources are not distributed uniformly. Per capita income in 1969 was below $3,000 in the poorest ten states, above $4,000 in the richest twelve.

A study by the Advisory Commission on Intergovernmental Relations has produced estimates of the revenues that a representative tax system, uniformly applied in all states, would yield.[1] This system, an average of U.S. state tax systems, would have yielded from $231 to $325 per capita in the top eight states, from $115 to $144 in the bottom eight states. Yet, some of the poorest states have particularly large numbers of school children and destitute families, hence the greatest fiscal needs.

Because the states and local communities continue to be responsible for the quality of such basic public services as education and because their financial situation has been precarious in recent years, several significant proposals have been advanced to help them.

[1] Advisory Commission on Intergovernmental Relations, *Measures of State and Local Fiscal Capacity and Tax Effort* (October 1962), p. 54.

A committee of governors and federal officials was appointed by President Eisenhower back in the 1950s to explore the possibility of changing the division of responsibility among the levels of government and adjusting the revenue system correspondingly. This group recommended, after studying many programs, that responsibility for vocational education and for waste-treatment facilities be returned to the states and that a part of the federal telephone tax be repealed in order to be reimposed by the states. This modest plan, which surrendered considerably more federal revenues than the costs of the programs, was turned down by the Congress. It was interesting that this group was not able to come up with more ambitious proposals. It turned out that the distribution of the benefits of returning a tax to the states was always different from the distribution of the costs of the programs; the states that would acquire more costs than tax revenues would be opposed. Furthermore, the officials managing the programs were fearful that the states would not allocate the newly gained revenues to the programs, letting quality deteriorate instead. Thus, when the issue of turning functions back to the states was put to the test of the political process, it turned out that people were content to leave things as they are.

Growth of Programmatic Grants-in-Aid

The initial solution to the problem of imbalance between federal and local finances was to greatly expand the various programs of grants for specific purposes. Many such programs have existed for decades. But beginning in the mid–1950s with the adoption of the multibillion dollar interstate highway program, the growth of grants with specific, usually narrowly defined purposes, became rapid indeed. Compared to $3 billion in 1955, grants to state and local governments reached $27 billion in 1971.

There are several types of programmatic grants-in-aid. Some are matching grants, in which the federal government puts up, say 50 percent of the funds, provided the state government raises the other 50 percent; this leaves part of the cost with the state and results in some weighing of taxes against the benefits of the expenditures. In other cases, grants may pay fixed amounts according to complicated formulas; for example, federal grants for public assistance may pay $25 of the first $30 per month plus half of the next $30 for each recipient. This helps assure that a minimum standard is reached in all states.

Programmatic grants are usually given only if numerous conditions are met. Some are specified by the Congress, others by bureaucratic regulation. Besides such conditions as compliance with civil service retirement systems and equal opportunity rules, elaborate plans must usually be submitted and numerous reports filed.

38

The conditional grants-in-aid in support of specific programs generally do advance the national objectives they are designed to serve. Our national highway system is immensely improved; public assistance is available at some minimum level everywhere; education, health, and science are being promoted. The disturbing question to which no answer has been provided so far is the effect of this great proliferation of specific programs on the state and local governments. As they rely more on federal financing, always in a rather directed form, with many conditions attached and often according to quite complex formulas, state and local activities are molded excessively to obtain the grants. Many a superhighway has been built, often roughshod through existing neighborhoods, because virtually all the financing could be obtained from the federal government. And those poor families that fall within the categories that are aided by the federal public assistance program (the aged, the disabled, the blind, and families with dependent children), are treated far more generously than the poor outside those categories, such as the working poor who are unable to earn an adequate income.

A Federal Tax Credit against State Income Taxes

One of the limitations to the ability of the states to raise revenue is the competition among them to attract industry through low tax rates. This competition has kept taxes on business income low and has also limited the growth of state personal income taxes.

To help state finances and to reduce this competition, the Advisory Commission on Intergovernmental Relations has proposed that the federal government give individual taxpayers a partial credit against their personal income taxes paid to states. For example, if an individual paid $100 to his state, he would be allowed to credit, say, one-half of that amount against his federal income tax, cutting his liability by $50. In effect, the federal government would pay half of state income taxes. Such a tax credit would provide an incentive to the states to introduce or raise personal income taxes because it would be a revenue source into which their own population would pay only half the total cost. It might also make states less sensitive to the pressures of interstate competition because only half of the cost would actually have to be paid by their own residents.

The impact of such a tax credit could be large. State income tax collections in 1969 were $10 billion. A 50 percent credit would reduce federal tax collections by $5 billion. If one assumes that states raise their tax rates correspondingly, they could gain $5 billion without imposing any additional cost on their own people.

But there are telling objections to this proposal. First, the benefit is particularly great in those states that have high incomes—and hence are able to collect much income tax on which to base the federal credit. Because the fiscal capacity of states is so uneven, it is desirable to make federal help available in an *equalizing* form—that is, to give relatively greater help to poor states. Second, there is no assurance that the states will actually raise their income tax rates to take advantage of the credit. Finally, the main thrust of the proposal is to put pressure

39

on the states to institute personal income taxation. States that have the tax receive a windfall; the dozen states that have chosen to do without an income tax would be pressed to participate in the windfall. But it is one of the ideas of our system of government to have states and localities free to choose their own methods of taxation: the tax credit is an intrusion of federal authority. For all these reasons, the tax credit idea has not taken hold.

Federal Revenue Sharing

The initial solution adopted by the federal government is a broad program of revenue sharing. The idea is remarkably simple: each year, the federal government distributes over $5 billion among the states according to a formula. Much of the money is distributed according to the population of each state. Although the distribution of these revenues is not equalizing, the collection of this money through the progressive federal income tax does serve to redistribute income in a progressive pattern. The formula is also designed to provide extra help for states that contain large metropolitan areas with their numerous social and physical problems. To assure that the states will pass appropriate sums on to their local governments, the law requires that each state distribute two-thirds of its received share to its localities. The states and localities are free to spend the money as they see fit with relatively few federal controls.

Revenue sharing has many advantages. It is a massive attempt to strengthen state and local governments. By leaving local governments free to spend the money on those programs for which they feel the most acute need, it strengthens local initiative and slows down the centralization of government. By adding to the total resources available to the states, the plan promotes the quality of public services, including particularly education, the greatest state and local responsibility. And finally, by reducing the pressure on the states and localities to raise property, gasoline, cigarette, and other nuisance taxes while relying more heavily on the more equitable federal income tax, the nation's tax system as a whole is maintained in better condition.

The main objections are these: despite our desire to strengthen the state and local governments, our confidence in them is not high. If state governments were given billions of dollars to spend as they saw fit, without strings, would they really spend it well?

Also, the plan separates the act of taxation from the act of spending in the political process. Taxation remains at the federal level, but spending decisions are in the hands of the states. It may be better to have the decision makers on the spending side confronted by the problems of raising the tax money to help assure efficiency and absence of waste.

SUMMARY

40

A federal, or multilevel, system of government has important advantages over a centralized system. It permits a greater diffusion of power, more sensitive choices about collective goods, the application of different values in programs in different regions and localities, and great opportunity for experimentation.

On the other hand, some of the most important public services deal with collective goods for the country as a whole, involving the national interest, and ought to be undertaken nationally. The federal government also has superior financial resources. Lack of local initiative makes us undertake some programs at the national level even though they really deal with local problems. Years of inquiries by presidential commissions and other groups have produced no results in returning functions to the states.

State and local expenditures have increased enormously in the postwar period. These expenditures have largely been financed out of state and local resources. Tax rates have been increased and new taxes adopted. Grant-in-aid programs from the federal government have also helped, but in a minor way.

The fiscal capacity of the 50 states varies widely, and this fact, together with the expectation of another doubling of local expenditures in the next ten years, has led to proposals to provide additional financial aid from the federal to state and local governments. In 1972, Congress enacted the first major revenue-sharing legislation, which provides $5 billion to the states and their localities.

Economics

of Metropolitan Areas

CHAPTER FOUR

Seventy percent of the American people now live in metropolitan areas. As defined by the Census Bureau, the country has 212 Standard Metropolitan Statistical Areas (SMSA) that range from the New York area with 12 million people, to areas with less than 100,000. Over 75 million live in areas of a size greater than 1 million; over 100 million in SMSAs greater than 500,000. Each area is a cluster of communities, usually consisting of a central core city plus surrounding suburbs. The growth of these areas and the large percentage of our population that now lives in them is a measure of the extent to which America has become urbanized (see Table 4–1).

Metropolitan areas have been defined not on the basis of legal boundaries of units of government, but according to their economic integration. People live and work within each area, but often not in the same town. People do their shopping, seek much of their recreation, and have their friends all within the area. Each area needs an efficient transportation system for the movement of people and goods at high speed and low cost. Most metropolitan areas are encountering serious difficulties in this task.

The communities in a metropolitan area have other common economic problems. A sensible division of the land among residential, commercial, industrial, and recreational uses requires an area-wide point of view. The general prosperity of the population depends not on the town alone but on the prosperity of the area as a whole. Often, public services such as sewers, hospitals, police and fire protection, and even libraries and schools can be provided more efficiently on an area-wide basis. They may be collective goods for the area as a whole, not just

42

collective to one community. Physical interdependence and external economies and diseconomies are the typical conditions. Hence, the benefits and costs confronted by the separate communities fail to fully measure the social benefits and costs for the area as a whole. As a result, the boundaries of the local governments within the metropolitan areas are not the proper boundaries for rational planning and decision making and for the efficient supply of many government services.

Metropolitan areas today pose some of the most interesting, not to say perplexing, problems in public finance. The important issues of local expenditures and taxation cannot meaningfully be considered without some analysis of the economics of metropolitan areas. This chapter will chiefly be concerned with one question: How can public services be organized most effectively in the modern metropolitan area?

TROUBLE IN THE CORE CITY

Our large cities, which are the heart of the metropolitan areas, have all experienced a gradual process of physical and economic deterioration. Manu-

Table 4–1 POPULATION GROWTH OF 24 STANDARD METROPOLITAN STATISTICAL AREAS WITH LARGEST POPULATION IN 1970

	Population (in thousands)	
	1900	1970
New York	4,718	11,529
Los Angeles–Long Beach	123	7,032
Chicago–NW Indiana	1,851	6,979
Philadelphia	1,623	4,818
Detroit	317	4,200
San Francisco–Oakland	473	3,110
Washington, D.C.–Md.–Va.	305	2,861
Boston	1,250	2,754
Pittsburgh	793	2,401
St. Louis, Mo.–Ill.	650	2,363
Baltimore	578	2,071
Cleveland	420	2,064
Houston	45	1,985
Newark	**	1,857
Minneapolis–St. Paul	372	1,814
Dallas	43	1,556
Seattle–Everett	81	1,422
Orange County, Calif.	**	1,420
Milwaukee	325	1,404
Atlanta	141	1,390
Cincinnati	496	1,385
Paterson–Clifton–Passaic, N.J.	**	1,359
San Diego	40	1,358
Buffalo	394	1,349

** Not a separate metropolitan area in 1900.

Source: Bureau of the Census.

43

facturing industry has been moving out. It had first been attracted to the city by the proximity of the railroads and a steady labor supply; but the rise of trucking, and now of airfreight, has made locations along major highways (and airports) outside the core city more attractive. This trend was accelerated by technical changes in factory buildings. Business found that modern one-story plants could operate at lower costs than the older multistory plants, but land values were too high in the city to make large one-story plants practical.

The cities have also been losing middle- and upper-income families to the suburbs. Partly a result of people's desire for more space and homeownership, this movement accelerated when the cities became caught in a vicious spiral of spreading slums, rising crime, and worsening congestion. Once a neighborhood began to deteriorate, it did not pay any one landlord to maintain his own building. If all landlords invested in the upkeep of their property, neighborhoods might be preserved. But once decline sets in, the private return on investment becomes small because little extra rent can be charged for the better kept-up buildings. This perhaps is the worst of the external diseconomies working against the preservation of our cities. The process was accentuated by the housing shortages after World War II, which made it easy to rent run-down apartments, and by the artificial shortage created by racial discrimination in housing, which preserves a captive market for dilapidated slum buildings in the large cities all over the United States. City schools have declined in quality and have been unable to meet the changing needs of the changing population. As a result, the tendency has been for only two groups of people to remain in the cities—the very rich who can afford to live in luxury apartments, especially if they are childless, and the poor, especially minorities, who have no choice but to live in the limited housing available to them and in close proximity to their unskilled service jobs.

This process has created a difficult financial situation for the cities. On the one hand, they have to bear public assistance payments and other welfare costs for the low-income groups in the slums, as well as to continue to provide mass transportation, fire and police protection, and education. On the other hand, their tax base has failed to expand correspondingly as high- and middle-income groups and industry fled the city.

PROBLEMS IN THE SUBURBS

Meantime, the burgeoning suburbs have developed some problems of their own. In some of them, population doubled and redoubled in a few years as developers put up moderate-scaled houses by the thousands. These communities had no financial resources of their own other than revenues from property taxes, and these were not equal to the enormous costs of providing schools and teachers for the numerous children of young families, as well as the heavy initial investments needed for water supply, roads, and sewers. Some towns have sought to broaden their tax base by attracting industry. But as towns have competed for

44

the new factories, they have made tax concessions that grant new industry partial exemption from the property taxes, thus reducing the total tax base of the area.

Taxes were high for other reasons as well. There are some costs involved in being a separate unit of government—the town hall, a salaried mayor or city manager, perhaps a local court. Some public services are carried on more efficiently on a larger scale and are costly for a small town. And unless there is active grass-roots democracy with heavy citizen participation and responsibility, local government may be inefficient because of the difficulty of attracting top-flight administrative talent.

While some suburbs suffered from mediocre schools and from high tax rates, others became "tax havens." They required house lots to be so large and made building codes so complicated that it became very difficult to build new houses and hence to add to the school population. By these and other devices, they kept themselves islands of low tax rates.

PROBLEMS OF COORDINATION AND PLANNING: PHYSICAL INTERDEPENDENCE IGNORED

The division of the metropolitan area into many legal communities makes it particularly difficult to provide those public services for which the metropolitan area has to be considered a unit for physical reasons. It makes no sense to plan transportation on other than an area-wide basis because of the typically long distances separating people's homes from their places of work. A rational road network must be able to move cars freely within the area. Mass-transit systems, subways or buses, also should be laid out on an area-wide basis. Yet, it is usually only the core city that feels it has sufficient stake in such a system to give it active support; the commuter suburbs are happy to have residents drive into the city and then to let the city worry about the congestion of streets and downtown parking.

Water supply is a similar problem. To obtain a supply of high quality water at low cost frequently requires the construction of a large reservoir at some distance up in the mountains. In the absence of unified area planning, localities improvise their own supplies, out of wells or other sources. The ground water level may gradually fall as supplies are depleted. The pumping process slowly raises pumping costs to the town and neighboring communities. Having made the investment in the pumping facilities, they are slow to abandon them, and are reluctant to participate in building a cheaper, better common system.

The disposal of sewage is an even worse case. Some suburbs, particularly if they have been growing rapidly and are straining their resources to finance schools, provide no sewers. Their home-owners use septic tanks that discharge waste material into the ground. Even if they have sewers, the contents may be discharged into neighboring streams rather than treatment plants. This process

45

has gone so far in some parts of the country that swimming at local beaches or streams has become impossible because of pollution. Even water supplies have been polluted by sewage seeping into the ground water.

These cases illustrate the point that the scope of particular governments must match the physical contours of the problems. Decentralization and local control are all very well, but not for the planning of water supplies and sewage disposal within a metropolitan area. When physical interdependence is ignored, decentralized decision making does not lead to efficient results. The costs that localities consider in their choices are not the full social costs to the area.

METROPOLITAN CONSOLIDATION?

Observers who have watched some of these difficulties, particularly officials struggling vainly to gain adherence to area-wide plans for common facilities, have frequently proposed that a new level of government be set up that would embrace the entire metropolitan area. Such a government could rationally plan highways and mass-transit facilities, water supplies and sewage disposal, parks and beaches, the location of schools, even civil defense. It could also impose a common level of taxation, and would end the possibility of upper-income people and industry fleeing into "tax havens." Equipped with an adequate tax base and a proper span of control, such a government could, at least in principle, deal properly with the many problems of coordinated physical planning and would have a better base for financing education and welfare programs. It could also supply some public services more efficiently.

Many of the issues involved in metropolitan consolidation are philosophical. Each person has to reach his own conclusion whether the improved planning and cost savings are worth the increased centralization. But two issues can be analyzed more concretely. First, how large are the economies of scale for the various public services; second, what alternative solutions are there that would permit some of the advantages to accrue without the disadvantages?

Several statistical studies have been made of the costs of public services in communities of different sizes. In a study of the communities in the area of St. Louis, Missouri,[1] it was found that there were no measurable economies of scale in police protection, fire protection, education, and refuse collection. Administrative services enjoyed economies of scale at least up to medium-sized communities of 50,000–100,000 persons. Water and sewage services exhibited important economies of scale, with no evidence of diseconomies even for the largest systems. Studies of this type cannot be wholly conclusive, because one can argue that the higher (or at least no lower) costs of education and other services of the large unit are due to higher quality (which we cannot measure precisely), so

[1] Werner Z. Hirsch, "Expenditure Implications of Metropolitan Growth and Consolidation," *Review of Economics and Statistics*, Vol. 41, August 1959, pp. 232–41.

that the taxpayer still receives more per dollar. But these studies do raise very serious doubts about across-the-board metropolitan consolidation justified primarily by economies of scale.

Apart from the statistical evidence, the efficiency argument for consolidation stumbles, at least in some places, on a more obvious obstacle. Many core-city governments, which could be expected to dominate the consolidated metropolitan area, are corrupt. To consolidate would mean to turn over well-run communities to the control of city machines. One can understand why suburbanites prefer some inefficiency and the costs of imperfect coordination to the prospect of falling under the sway of big-city politicians.

ALTERNATIVES
TO METROPOLITAN CONSOLIDATION

In fact, metropolitan consolidation has been carried out only to a very limited extent. Toronto, Canada, consolidated in 1952 and had a successful subsequent experience of improved services, better coordination, and cost savings. This example raised interest in the plan in other cities. Dade County, Florida, which has Miami as its core, was organized as a metropolitan government in 1957 and was given the tasks of supplying such public services as water, sewage, hospitals, welfare, parks, mass transit, urban renewal, and arterial roads. Nashville undertook a major consolidation in 1962. Elsewhere, as in Cleveland, St. Louis, Memphis, Albuquerque, and Louisville, voters defeated plans for consolidation even though these plans gave the proposed governments only limited functions. Typically, it was the resistance of the suburbs that defeated the proposals.[2]

In the absence of consolidation, other solutions have been found, which eliminate the worst anomalies of the lack of unified political responsibility for common problems. First, some economies of scale have been realized through voluntary cooperation of communities. Regional high schools, shared incinerators, and mutual assistance agreements among fire departments are quite common. Some towns buy services from other communities. This technique has been most developed in the Los Angeles area, where Los Angeles County is a department store of public services; each town can contract to purchase virtually any service it wishes. When the city of Lakewood was formed in 1954, it decided to contract for all its public services except education, and this scheme is now known as the "Lakewood Plan."

Second, new governments, sometimes called Metropolitan Special Districts, or Authorities, have been created to supply specific government services. For example, the Los Angeles Metropolitan Water District provides much of the

---

[2] Up to 1920, the cities were able to keep the metropolitan populations inside their boundaries by legally annexing the surrounding countryside. Local opposition brought this process to a halt.

water supply to Southern California. The New York Port Authority, in addition to managing the port and bus terminals, builds and operates tunnels, bridges, and airports. It has an annual investment budget of over $100 million, which it finances partly out of its very lucrative tunnel and bridge tolls and partly out of bonds issued on its own credit. The Seattle Metropolitan Municipal Corporation takes care of sewage and pollution control for its area. The Massachusetts Metropolitan District Commission supplies water, sewers, as well as some of the highways and parks of the greater Boston area. There are also many smaller special districts, supplying smaller regions with water, sewage, or some other service.

These governments have often proved efficient, although they are subject neither to the check of competition nor of the ballot box. They succeed in raising huge amounts of capital and seem to provide public services to the satisfaction of their customers. They pose more difficult issues as political organisms. Although they are governments, possessing the power of eminent domain and sometimes even of taxation, they are certainly not democracies. Their chiefs are not elected by the residents of the area and are frequently appointed for such long terms that no elective official has any real check over them. In fact, in some areas, the technocrats who run these agencies are the most powerful politicians. The facilities that they control, particularly tunnels, bridges, and toll roads, produce far more revenue than is required to repay the bonds on the specific facilities; the surplus becomes a pool of investible funds with which they search for new fields to conquer. With the regular governments perennially hard-pressed for tax money, more and more activities are turned over to them. America has not thought through the implications of this trend.

Third, some of the problems of metropolitan areas have been turned over to the federal government. The large cities particularly have found it impossible to cope with the problem of urban blight, as their tax resources have declined in relation to their mounting expenses. The various federal programs are a response to the failure or inability of local jurisdictions to take effective action. The federal highway program is providing an important share of the funds for building some of the main access arteries in metropolitan areas. The federal public assistance and other antipoverty programs are providing important financial help for the welfare problems of the large cities. Grants for the improvement of mass-transit systems have become available. Various community development programs allow cities to experiment with new approaches to their physical and human problems.

Until a few years ago, we did not view these urban problems in the perspective of total metropolitan areas. The radical solution of establishing a new level of government through metropolitan consolidation has not been, and is not likely to be, adopted widely. In some areas, we find *ad hoc* solutions, voluntary cooperation, new agencies, and a wholesale transfer of problems to the federal government. But these solutions are all piecemeal. They do not produce a rational, integrated transportation system for the metropolitan area as a whole, nor an equitable local tax system, nor a rational pattern of land use. We have a lot to learn in this area.

SUMMARY

Some of the most difficult problems of public finance today can be found in metropolitan areas. Because legal jurisdictions of governments do not coincide with economic boundaries, the proper provision of government services requires some cooperation, coordination, and some centralized planning.

Over 100 million people live in metropolitan areas with a population in excess of 500,000 people. The typical area contains a cluster of communities surrounding the central core city.

The core cities have been running into economic difficulties because of physical and economic deterioration. Industry and middle- and upper-income families have been leaving, eroding the tax base. Slums have sprung up as the private benefit of proper maintenance of apartment dwellings has fallen short of social benefit. It does not pay any one landlord to keep up his buildings as long as the rest of the neighborhood runs downhill.

Suburbs with rapidly rising populations have run into severe financial problems. Their tax resources are small in relation to their needs for new schools, water, roads, and sewers. In some instances, individual suburbs are too small to be able to supply government services efficiently.

Decentralized planning cannot work properly if communities are physically interdependent. Transportation, water supply, and sewage disposal are three public services in which physical interdependence is particularly important and in which an area-wide point of view is essential.

Consolidating communities in a metropolitan area under one government has been proposed to eliminate these problems. But so far, voters have rejected metropolitan consolidation in most popular referenda. Statistical studies suggest that economies of scale prevail for some services, particularly water and sewage. But for many others, including education, there are little or no economies of scale, and hence fewer gains from metropolitan consolidation.

To realize some of the advantages of consolidation without taking this major political step, a number of alternative arrangements have been introduced. These include voluntary cooperation among communities to provide common facilities; the "Lakewood Plan," under which communities can contract to purchase those government services that they feel they cannot produce efficiently themselves; and Metropolitan Special Districts, which are area-wide governments limited to providing certain specific government services.

The federal government has also been taking increasing responsibility for problems of urban areas, particularly through its urban renewal and highway and antipoverty programs.

49

Taxation: Principles
and Issues of Fairness

CHAPTER FIVE

Perhaps the most astonishing fact about the American tax system is the fantastic revenue that it collects; total taxes are over $300 billion, about 29 percent of gross national product. They are collected without violence or bloodshed, with only some mild griping.

This is a small miracle. It is possible because in our advanced society businesses and individuals keep accounting records from which they can compute their tax bill. More important, it is possible because, on the whole, people are willing to pay their taxes. Ours is a system of voluntary compliance, not of assessment and enforcement by government. Less than 3 percent of the federal government's revenues are the direct result of Internal Revenue Service findings of underpayments. People know that the common costs of national defense, of educating our children, and of other necessary public services have to be met. Generally, people respect the law and pay their taxes.

For a voluntary system to work successfully, the people must be confident that taxes are levied fairly and that everyone pays his share. If the feeling becomes widespread that the tax system is simply a collection of loopholes and evasions, if people see their equally prosperous neighbors paying substantially less or enjoying tax-free expense-account living, taxpayer morale declines. The submission of an honest tax return then ceases to be a simple act of morality. In many countries of the world, both rich and poor, ethics concerning taxes are separate from ethics in other spheres. In Italy and France, countries of old culture, the most respectable members of the business and professional classes will report a taxable income that is no more than a fraction of their true income. Businesses routinely keep two sets of books, one for their own use, the other for the tax collectors. We have been spared this Latin tradition. Willingness to pay taxes is one of the sources of our national strength. The fairness of our taxes, which is essential to the maintenance of our voluntary compliance system, is the central theme of this chapter.

The magnitude of the revenues raised also means that the economy as a whole is affected. These enormous payments cannot leave the efficiency, growth, and stability of the economy entirely unchanged. How these payments affect the economy will be discussed in subsequent chapters.

TAX BASES AND TAX RATES

Every tax is composed of a base and of a rate structure applied to that base. The base is the object that is taxed. It may be personal or business income, the sale of salt (an important base in the Middle Ages) or of other commodities, the total volume of sales of a business, the value of property, the estate left by an individual, the crossing of goods over a frontier (tariffs), and so on. This base may be taxed at a flat rate, such as a percentage of value or a fixed amount per physical unit, or with a more elaborate rate structure, such as the progressive income tax rates.

SHIFTING AND INCIDENCE

Frequently, a tax is collected from one individual, while in fact it is someone else who pays. By adjusting his actions, the taxed individual may be able to escape part of the burden and shift it to someone else. For example, the federal tax on cigarettes is collected from the manufacturers, yet they do not really pay most of the tax. They raise the price of the cigarettes, so that they *shift* the tax *forward* to the consumer, who pays the tax through higher prices. The *incidence*—that is, the final resting place of the tax burden—in this case falls on the consumer. To some extent, the tax also may lower the demand for tobacco, resulting in a lower price paid to tobacco growers. Thus, a little of the tax may be *shifted backward*, placing some of the incidence on the growers.

The process of shifting can be analyzed through the supply and demand mechanism. (Figure 5–1). Let S and D be the supply and demand curves of a commodity. The initial equilibrium price is p_1, the equilibrium quantity is q_1. Now, suppose an excise tax of a fixed amount per unit is imposed. Then, the supply curve shifts upward by the amount of the tax; that is, to obtain any given amount of the good, buyers must offer a greater price, including tax, to draw forth the supply. But at higher prices, they demand less, and so a new equilibrium is found at q_2, where consumers pay p_2, producers receive p_3, and the difference between p_2 and p_3 is the tax that goes to the government.

51

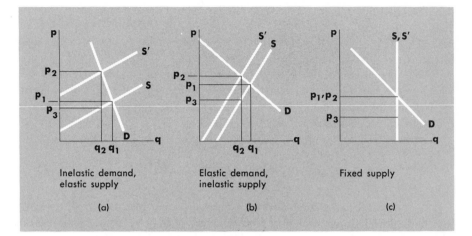

FIG. 5-1 Shifting and incidence of an excise tax.

In example (a), the larger part of the tax was passed on in a higher price, the smaller part was absorbed by the producers. But suppose the demand were a lot more elastic, and the supply less elastic, as in (b). Then, more of the incidence falls on the suppliers. In the limiting case where the supply is completely inelastic (that is, fixed), the whole of the tax will fall on the suppliers, as in example (c). Conversely, if the demand is completely inelastic, the tax will be completely shifted forward.

These diagrams illustrate rather general principles. If demand is elastic, either because the good is not important to the buyer or there are ready substitutes for it, then the buyer will easily shift the tax to the suppliers by curtailing his purchases. If supply is elastic—if producers can readily shift factors into other lines of production—then the newly taxed commodity will not fall much in the price received by producers, and the tax will remain on the buyers.

It is clear enough that excise taxes on specific goods can, at least in part, be shifted. But the question also arises in connection with other taxes. Who really pays the corporation income tax? Does it all come out of the profits of the companies? Or is some of it shifted forward in higher prices? And is a part shifted backward into lower wages? Do individuals pay all the personal income taxes levied on them? We will return to these difficult questions later on. Without facing up to the possible shifting and the resultant incidence of the various taxes, it is impossible to evaluate the fairness of this system or its impact on the economy's performance.

PRACTICAL CRITERIA
FOR TAX SYSTEMS

52

Both for the sake of fairness and to minimize the damage done to the economy, a tax system should display sound administrative qualities. These include:

Certainty

For a private economy to operate successfully, it needs a stable political environment, including a tax system under which payments are predictable. Investment is risky under the best of circumstances, and if business is uncertain about the amount of tax that is to be paid, investment will be reduced. Similarly, individuals should be secure against unpredictable taxes levied on their wages or other incomes. The law should be clear and specific; tax collectors should have little discretion about how much to assess taxpayers, for this is a very great power and subject to abuse.

In our present tax system, the property tax based on arbitrary local assessments of value is probably the most uncertain tax, and for this reason leads to a great deal of friction, substantial inequity among property-owners, a reduction of investment in buildings, and, no doubt, to some corruption.

Compliance and Collection Costs

Because the compliance costs to the taxpayers and the collection costs to the government add nothing to the national output, resources should not be wasted on them. Our major taxes have fairly low compliance and collection costs today, a few percent of total revenue at most. But there are exceptions. State taxes on corporation income, which often furnish little revenue, force companies that do business in many states to maintain elaborate business records not needed for other business purposes. For example, the assistant treasurer of a stove company reports that four employees (one-sixth of the total accounting department) were required to prepare some 282 separate state, county, and municipal tax returns. Their cost, plus legal and accounting services, was $39,000 a year. The total taxes paid were only $74,000, so that the compliance cost to the company was over half the amount of the taxes. These costs could be cut if all states accepted a uniform system of returns and agreed on simple formulas for allocating business income to each state.

Enforceability

A good tax system does not impose taxes that are impossible to enforce. Even where voluntary compliance is the rule, the possibility of verifying tax payments must exist; otherwise, the tax becomes an invitation to break the law. Some of the deductions permitted under the federal income tax lead to this kind of situation. Local taxes and charitable contributions can be deducted from income. But who keeps track of every penny of gasoline taxes or every dollar he gives to the dozens of charity drives? Without records, people make a crude estimate that the government cannot check. The result: a temptation to be more generous in estimating than in giving. In our advanced society, a great many taxes can be enforced; but in less-developed countries, where there is less record keeping and many people are illiterate, the possibilities of enforceable taxation are much more circumscribed.

53

Most important is that the tax system should be acceptable to the public. It should be consistent with people's notions of fair play and should not be too onerous compared to what they get for their tax dollars.

A FAIR TAX SYSTEM:
CRITERIA OF EQUITY

What we mean by a fair system is not a question of technical economics but of personal philosophy. Nevertheless, some principles have been developed over the years and provide a useful framework. These are the benefit principle and the principle of ability to pay. Most discussion and controversy about equity is conducted within that framework.

The *benefit principle* calls for a distribution of taxes in accordance with the benefits received from the expenditures on which the taxes are spent. People pay for the goods and services received in the private economy, so why not in the public sector? If taxation violates the benefit principle, then public services are a form of subsidy for their users, because the services are received at other people's expense.

The benefit principle is, in fact, applied to highway taxation, where road building is paid by earmarked highway-user taxes, set aside in separate accounts from which they cannot be "diverted" to other purposes. The principle is also applied in the social-security field, where the payroll taxes are earmarked for the reserves from which the benefit payments are made. Many local services, such as the construction of sewers and streets, are partly financed out of special assessments levied on the residents who will be served.

Although fairness is one of the basic ideas behind these applications of the benefit principle, this form of taxation also provides a substitute for the market test. After all, if the people who will benefit from expenditures are not willing to pay for them through their taxes, presumably they are not worth their cost and should not be undertaken.[1]

The benefit principle can be applied only where the beneficiaries can be clearly identified. This is not true of most public services. How is the benefit of national defense or of education to be divided among the population? Thus, at best, the principle can provide a partial solution to the problem of fairness in taxation.

The *ability-to-pay principle* is the other standard of fairness. Adam Smith, back in 1776, listed this as the first canon of taxation, and most people take it

[1] The test of value is very crude because total revenues are compared with total cost and no tests are performed at the margin.

for granted that a fair tax system calls on the richer members of the community to pay more taxes than the poor.

Actually, the ability-to-pay principle has two separate parts. It states not only that the rich should pay more but also that those who are similarly situated (for example, have the same income) should pay the same taxes. This second idea, that "equals be treated equally," is called *horizontal equity*; the proper division of the tax burden among people of different ability to pay is called *vertical equity*. Many of the practical issues of tax equity that are before the Congress are appeals for horizontal equity—all too often the request for a special tax privilege by one group because another enjoys it.

MEASURES OF ABILITY TO PAY: THE CHOICE OF TAX BASE

It is one thing to agree that taxes be levied according to ability to pay, but another to agree on the measure of this ability. We usually think of income as the best measure, for it determines a person's total command over resources during a stated period to consume or to add to his wealth. The late Henry Simons of the University of Chicago, perhaps the outstanding thinker on this problem, argued that all taxes, whatever their nominal base, ought to be considered to fall on individual incomes. When all the shifting is done, every tax is paid by somebody, and does, in fact, reduce that individual's income. Simons wanted to create a tax system with perfect horizontal equity in which the people with the same incomes would pay the same taxes, and with vertical equity also income based. This ideal tax system would have required getting rid of most of the taxes other than income taxes, but would have made the definition of income truly comprehensive, including gifts, inheritances, and transfer payments.

Wealth might also be considered an appropriate measure of ability to pay. Although, in a sense, it would be double taxation to tax both income and wealth because the wealth produces income (which is taxed), nevertheless the mere possession of wealth may yield satisfaction on its own. Historically, the U.S. has been as much concerned with an excessive concentration of wealth as of income. Our estate and gift taxes are a response to this concern.

Another approach has been advanced by Nicholas Kaldor of Cambridge, England. He has advocated what he calls an expenditure tax, a tax on consumption.[2] He argues that consumption rather than income should be the proper base of taxation. It is consumption that measures the resources that an individual actually withdraws from the economy for his personal use. The part of his income not consumed, his savings, adds to the country's capital stock and serves to raise total productive capacity; if an individual chooses to consume more than his income (by buying on credit or drawing on his past savings) he should pay

[2] Nicholas Kaldor, *An Expenditure Tax* (London: Allen and Unwin), 1955.

55

a higher tax because he is depleting the capital stock of the country. This idea is particularly attractive in underdeveloped countries where high consumption levels of the richer classes may make private capital accumulation small. An expenditure tax would discourage consumption by taxing it heavily and encourage savings by granting it tax exemption. Such a tax could be progressive, with rates rising with the total amount spent by an individual on consumption.[3]

In actual practice, governments use a great variety of tax bases. Personal and corporate income are the most important tax bases at our federal level; state and local governments rely more heavily on property, sales, and excise taxes. The variety of tax bases is a result of governments' perennial need for more money. When expenditures increase more than the revenue produced by the tax system, governments look for new sources, which usually means new tax bases. Excessive reliance on any one base may produce adverse economic effects because the rates may become too high. Therefore, a tax system may do less economic damage if it raises moderate amounts from several bases rather than large amounts from one or two.

VERTICAL EQUITY:
THE STRUCTURE OF TAX RATES

Adam Smith argued that taxes should be *proportional* to income— that is, that everybody should pay the same percentage of his income as taxes. Today, we have gone one step further. We favor *progressive* taxes, which means that the fraction of income paid increases as income rises, so that the increase in tax payments is more than proportionate. This is the opposite of a *regressive* tax, under which the fraction of income paid declines as income rises.

Our tax system today is a mixture of all three kinds of taxes. The personal income tax is progressive, of course, with a tax rate of zero on the first $750 of income and a rate structure rising to 70 percent. But many other taxes are regressive, such as the heavy excises on gasoline, tobacco, and liquor. Take the tax on cigarettes, for example. A person with a high income is not going to smoke much more than a poor man, and even if he finds an expensive, exotic brand, the tax will be no greater because it is levied on the physical quantity, not on value. We also have some proportionate taxes. State sales taxes, particularly where they exempt food, are just about proportionate. So are the property taxes, which are still much the most important tax at the state and local level.

[3] But think of the administrative problems. Every taxpayer would need to have records of his consumption expenditures, or else of his total income and the change in his wealth. Kaldor favors the second method. He would require taxpayers to submit both a balance sheet and an income statement as part of their tax return. Net additions on the balance sheet would reflect savings. The tax would be levied on income minus the net additions to wealth, which should correspond to consumption if the accounting is done precisely. Because of the administrative difficulties, the tax was tried in only two countries, India and Ceylon, and their experience was not satisfactory.

Taking the American tax system as a whole, is it progressive or regressive? This question is difficult to answer, because we not only have to know the composition of the tax system, but we also have to make some assumptions about the final incidence of each tax—that is, to what extent the taxes are shifted and to whom. Professor Musgrave has prepared careful estimates of the total incidence of our tax system, using what seemed to him the most reasonable incidence assumptions about each tax. Estimates based on 1965 data are shown in Fig. 5–2. You will notice that there is rather little progression from the low incomes through the middle-income range. Up to that point, the regressive excise and property taxes offset the progressive income taxes. In the upper incomes, the income tax becomes more important, to the point where it makes the tax structure as a whole progressive. As you would expect, the state and local tax systems, with their heavy reliance on sales, excise, and property taxes, are slightly regressive all the way up the income scale.

THE FEDERAL
PERSONAL INCOME TAX

We rely on the progressive federal income tax to assure a fair distribution of the tax burden. It is our main policy instrument for reducing the inequality of the distribution of income in our society. The rate structure remains

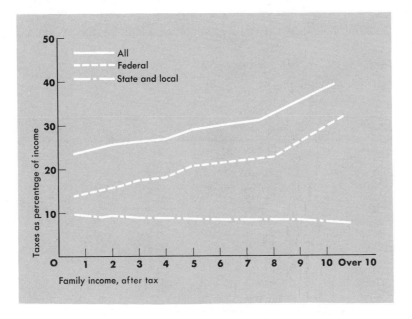

FIG. 5–2 Burden of the U.S. tax system by income class, 1965. (Source: Tax Foundation.)

progressive (See Table 5–1), although various provisions blunt the impact of the step rates.

The tax is levied on "all income, from whatever source derived," according to the Internal Revenue Code, but there are some important exceptions called *exclusions*. Government transfer payments such as social security benefits, gifts and inheritances, and most incomes in kind (the benefit of homeownership, on-the-farm food consumption) are not included in the legal income concept, called *adjusted gross income*. On the other hand, the legal definition includes much of the necessary cost of earning a living, such as commuting expenses, lunch money, and the cost of dressing appropriately for the job, even though some of these items may reduce the income available for family consumption or saving.

Our tax system recognizes that income is not the only factor in economic welfare. It therefore permits *deductions* of numerous items from adjusted gross income. The most important of these are:

1. Taxes paid to local governments
2. Interest payments
3. Medical expenses above 3 percent of income
4. Contributions to charity
5. Casualty losses, such as losses from fire and theft

If the taxpayer chooses not to claim itemized deductions, he can claim a *standard deduction* of 15 percent of his income, up to $2,000 per couple. Any family is assured a minimum deduction, called a low income allowance, which can be as high as $1,000.

In addition, the law permits *exemptions*, $600 for the taxpayer and for

Table 5–1 FEDERAL INCOME TAX RATES FOR A MARRIED COUPLE WITH TWO CHILDREN[1]

Family Income Before Tax ($)	Personal Income Tax ($)	Family Income After Tax ($)	Average Tax Rate (%)	Marginal Tax Rate (%)
3,000	0	3,000	0	0
5,000	178	4,822	4	15
8,000	586	7,414	7	17
10,000	905	9,095	9	19
15,000	1,820	13,180	12	22
25,000	4,380	20,620	18	32
50,000	14,560	35,440	29	48
100,000	42,180	57,820	42	60
200,000	107,530	82,470	54	69
500,000	317,480	182,520	63	70
1,000,000	667,480	333,520	67	70
5,000,000	3,467,480	1,532,520	69	70

[1] The table assumes the law effective beginning in 1973, with $750 exemption for husband and wife, 15% standard deduction up to $2,000, or low income allowance.

each of his dependents, plus an extra exemption for people over 65 and the blind. The exemption is based on the bare cost of subsistence, an amount therefore left immune from taxation.[4]

The income tax was adopted in 1913 but remained at low rates until 1940. Since then, the rate structure has been highly progressive, with a maximum rate in excess of 90 percent in effect most of the time. This extreme progression was adopted at the beginning of World War II in order to take the profit out of war, at a time when there was even consideration of an absolute income ceiling of $25,000 that anyone could keep after taxes. These rates were more extreme than the American people really wanted; the spirit of egalitarianism is not that strong in the United States. In fact, there were enough loopholes in the tax structure to keep actual rates substantially lower. The average effective tax rates— that is, the actual tax paid divided by adjusted gross income, did not exceed 50 percent in any income bracket, even when income exceeded $1 million.

The tax reforms of 1964 eliminated the very high progressive rates, establishing the nominal rate structure at from 14 percent to 70 percent. The tax reform of 1969 imposed a 50 percent ceiling on the tax of earned income. The actual effective tax rates have been substantially lower, not exceeding 40 percent in any income bracket and with the latest reductions will be lower still.

ISSUES OF FAIRNESS
IN THE PERSONAL INCOME TAX

Erosion of the Tax Base?

Observers have pointed out that so many exclusions, exemptions, and deductions have crept into the tax system that the tax base has shrunk to a point where it is only half of personal income. Besides personal exemptions, such deductions as state and local taxes, charitable contributions, medical and dental expenses, and interest paid by households reduce taxable income. Table 5–2, which merits your close study, summarizes this phenomenon for the year 1968. If the tax base were not so narrow, just $353 out of $689 billion, the rate structure could be lower. In the sense that the numerous special provisions have narrowed the tax base and forced us to retain higher rates to raise the necessary revenues, they have been self-defeating.

Base-broadening reform is difficult to enact because every one of the exclusions, deductions, and exemptions was put into the tax law for a specific purpose, to relieve some particular inequity or to respond to some particular pressure.

---

[4] The law also permits some *tax credits*, specific reductions of tax liability. So far, this has been a minor device in the United States, the only current uses being (1) a retirement income credit, a complicated provision designed to give equal treatment to retired persons living on pensions but not receiving tax-exempt social-security benefits; (2) credits against foreign income taxes; and (3) the investment credit discussed in Chapter Six.

Table 5-2   EROSION OF THE TAX BASE, 1968 (billions of dollars)

Personal income (national income accounts)		689
—Exclusions from personal income		135
—Transfer payments	57	
—Supplements to wages and salaries (fringe benefits)	23	
—Income in kind (mainly homeownership)	37	
—Nonreported income	45	
+Employee contributions to social security	23	
+Miscellaneous (taxed half of capital gains, etc.)	15	
=Adjusted gross income		554
—Adjusted gross income on nontaxable returns		16
—Deductions		85
—Exemptions		104
=Taxable income		353
Tax		68

Thus, a rehabilitation of the tax base requires reversing previous successful campaigns by various groups to get preferential treatment. Those same groups defend their privileges. You may want to go through the list yourself and decide in your own mind which exclusions, deductions, exemptions, and credits you believe to be just.

Is the Tax System Too Generous to Homeowners?

The system of deductions is particularly favorable to homeownership. Two of the biggest expenses of owning a house are the payment of local taxes and interest on the mortgage, both of which are deductible; other fields of consumption do not offer comparable tax savings. Capital invested in a home earns a tax-free return because we do not tax the income-in-kind stemming from the use of the home. In contrast, a renter, who puts his capital into securities, pays taxes on the income and pays his rent out of after-tax income.

But there are social and political considerations to be weighed also. We really like to encourage homeownership, which is said to make people more stable and secure. Also, the deduction of local taxes from the federal tax base is a long-established principle of our multilevel system of government. Without this deduction, opposition to local taxes would be greater, and local services, including education, would suffer. Thus, this deduction takes some of the sting out of the local tax burdens and helps the financial position of states and localities.

The Special Treatment of Capital Gains

If a person makes money in the stock market or realizes other gains from having his capital assets become more valuable, he will not be taxed at the regular personal income tax rates, provided he has held the asset at least six months. Instead, he pays tax on only half the gain, in effect, cutting the tax rates in half. The unrealized gain on assets continuing to be held are not taxed at all. This is obviously a very powerful tax provision, accounting for a large part of the gap between the nominal and the effective tax rates in the upper brackets. At the top of the income scale, it means the difference between keeping 30 cents out of a dollar of ordinary income and keeping 65 cents out of a dollar of capital gain.[5] And even that tax need only be paid if the gain is realized.

The gap between capital gains rates and ordinary income rates is the central feature of many tax loopholes. For example, stock options are in wide use as a means of paying top-level executives. A company gives its vice-president, *A*, the option to purchase a thousand shares of its common stock at a price of $35, an option that he can exercise any time, say, during three years. Suppose the stock rises to $45; *A* exercises the option, buys the thousand shares at $35, holds them for a few years during which time the price of stock stays constant, and then sells it. He has made $10,000, which is a capital gain, taxable at half the usual rate.

The stock option was originally used in order to give professional managers an ownership stake in the business, to make their interests coincide with those of the stockholders. But under the pressure of the tax laws, more and more stock options were given to executives as a form of income subject to favorable tax treatment. Congress has tightened the rules, but they remain an important loophole.

Capital gains have been used in other ways to furnish relief from the regular rates. The sale of timber, livestock, and some mineral rights is accorded the favored capital gains treatment; so is the sale of a patent, an incentive to inventors.

Capital gains also reduce the degree of competition of the economy. A man who has built up a business, perhaps through a successful new product, may be unable, because of the progressive income and estate taxes, to pass on the benefits to his family except by selling out. The family may also have no way to pay the estate tax because it cannot liquidate part of the business to pay the tax. The entrepreneur sells out to a larger company. As a result, he reaps a capital gain, pays the lower tax, and puts the money into securities. The result is that another independent business has disappeared.

The present system has questionable economic characteristics. It penalizes earned income such as wages and salaries, while giving a tax break to incomes that qualify as capital gains. It also has the effect of making corporation stockholders more anxious to have stock appreciate in value rather than to yield dividends. This has discouraged the payment of dividends and led major corporations to retain their earnings. They rely on these internal funds for investment and do not need to compete for funds in the open capital market. We rely on markets to allocate resources efficiently. The allocation of investment is particu-

---

[5] The tax can be escaped altogether as long as the asset is not sold. Only capital gains "realized" in a market transaction are subject to tax. It has been estimated that over half of all capital gains are never realized during people's lifetimes. Upon the transfer of the asset at death, assets are revalued, and any gains achieved up to that date cease to be subject to income tax.

larly critical to the growth and efficiency of the economy. Yet, the tax system has helped to create a situation where most business investment does not go through the market test.

Why do we give such favorable treatment to capital gains? I believe there are three reasons: (1) People do not seem to consider capital gains exactly like other income. They are "paper profits" that people frequently put back into other securities rather than include in their regular household budgets. People separate their thinking about capital and about income, and even though an increase in the value of a person's wealth is income under most reasonable definitions, people may nevertheless think of it as a part of their capital accounts, as something to be reinvested rather than consumed. (2) A well-functioning capitalist system requires that not all capital accumulation take place inside corporations. Individuals should also be able to accumulate capital and make it available in an open market, where new and expanding firms can compete for it. Under the full progressive income tax rates, it would be difficult for substantial amounts of capital to accumulate in private hands. Thus, we sacrifice some fairness in the tax system to maintain a healthy system of private capital accumulation. (3) Capital gains are the rewards for successful risk-taking. We do not allow unlimited deductions for losses, so some favorable tax treatment for gains is justified to keep investment from becoming a "Heads you win, tails I lose" proposition.

Tax Shelters

A tax shelter is a device that permits the taxpayer to plow back earnings on capital without their being subject to tax, at least until such time as he removes the capital for his personal use. Because of our desire to facilitate capital accumulation, we have allowed, perhaps even encouraged, the widespread use of tax shelters.

Company pension plans are a prime example. The money paid into a pension plan by a company is not considered income to the employee until he has retired and the pension is being paid out. Thus, the capital can accumulate inside the pension fund over the working life of the employee without being taxed. Furthermore, a person's income after retirement is likely to be less than it was during his working years, so the rate at which the pension will be taxed will presumably be lower.

The self-employed, such as lawyers, doctors, and owners of small businesses, cannot participate in these company pension plans and therefore find it more difficult to accumulate wealth to provide for their retirement years. On the one hand, it is only fair to provide them with the same opportunities that corporations employees enjoy under the tax laws. On the other hand, this is a perfect example of eroding the tax base in the name of horizontal equity. What starts as the preferential treatment of one group becomes extended to other groups who claim that they are entitled to the same privilege. In 1962, after years of lobbying, Congress gave the self-employed the privilege of setting up their own pension plans with tax shelter privileges, though only for limited amounts and hedged by numerous restrictions.

Life insurance is another important tax shelter. The reserves built up by each policy are allowed to earn interest without being taxed to the individual until such time as the policy is paid off. If the policy pays off at death, it permanently escapes income taxation.

Tax-Exempt Securities

The interest on the bonds of state and local governments has traditionally been exempt from federal income taxation. As a result, individuals in very high tax brackets can purchase these securities to earn a tax-free income. The bonds consequently have been bid up in price, so that a good quality local bond yields less than a U.S. government bond. This has greatly facilitated the debt-financing of the rapidly rising state and local expenditures.

In earlier years, the interest yield on the bonds was bid so low that this loophole had little value. No tax was paid but not much interest was collected. But as the volume of local debt has kept on increasing by leaps and bounds, the premium on the bonds has shrunk, so that today many of the tax-free bonds yield interest close to the rates of savings accounts. Thus, the benefit to the localities becomes smaller, while the benefit to the purchasers grows. Local governments wish to retain this marketing aid for their bonds and to remain free of the potential federal control that goes with taxation.

The Problem of Uneven Incomes

People whose incomes are bunched into a small part of their working life, such as professional athletes, entertainers, and authors of best-sellers, are treated harshly by the tax law. In the brief years in which they earn their large incomes, they are subject to the highly progressive tax rates. Were they to earn the same amount of money in a more even pattern, they would pay substantially less. A ballplayer who earns a modest income for a few years, then becomes a major league star, earning perhaps $50,000 a year, and reverts to a modest income when his playing days are over, may pay in taxes almost half of what he earned during his best years. Someone else, receiving the same total revenue but in the more typical gradually rising lifetime pattern, will pay much less.

To remedy this inequity, people in these categories are allowed to "average" their incomes. This enables them to compute their tax liability as if the income were earned, not in one year, but spread evenly over five years. If one year's income exceeds the average of the previous four years by more than a third and also by a minimum of $3,000, the progression of the tax rates applied to that excess is reduced considerably below normal.

63

FAIRNESS IN OTHER TAXES

Although most of the controversy about fairness centers on the personal income tax, the other types of taxes also raise some equity questions. I mention only a few common types of issues.

Estate and Gift Taxes

The U.S. has highly progressive estate and gift taxes. The first $60,000 of an estate are exempt. The rates start at 3 percent, reach 18 percent at $100,000, 39 percent at $1 million, and 77 percent at $10 million.[6] Even more than in the case of the income tax, there are numerous means of avoiding the tax. The legal provisions are extremely complicated, and the impact of the tax on an estate is capricious, depending partly on the amount of effort and legal skill that has gone into the planning of the estate. Estate taxes are levied not just because wealth is a measure of ability to pay but also to prevent the concentration of wealth in a few hands. The existence of enormous family fortunes and their survival over the generations shows that the present taxes are ineffective in achieving these objectives.

The major avenue of avoidance is the establishment of family trusts. These are legal entities that may hold property, pay out some of the income to family members over their lifetimes, and distribute the property to the beneficiaries a generation or two later. In this way, the estate tax can be skipped by one or two generations and the family wealth is kept intact.

The estate and gift taxes are a real test of the extent of egalitarianism in the society's political preferences. The concentration of wealth has long been recognized to be much sharper than the concentration of income. Yet, the reform of these taxes has been far down on the agenda for political action, and no major reforms were included in the two overhauls of the tax system in the 1960s. More recently, public discussion has begun to focus on reforming these taxes.

Preferential Treatment for Some Industries
Under the Corporation Income Tax

Although most industries pay the full 48 percent of their profits as federal corporation income tax, a few receive preferential treatment. The natural-resource industries, particularly crude-oil producers, pay lower rates because of the *depletion allowance*. On the theory that the sale of minerals is not like the sale of the output of an ordinary business but rather involves the sale of a company's assets, the Congress, back in 1913, allowed these industries to deduct a

[6] Gift tax rates are 75 percent of the estate rates and are mainly designed to prevent escape from the estate tax through gifts before death.

small percentage of their total revenue from their taxable income as a depletion allowance. Over the years, this percentage has been increased, and similar allowances have been extended to other minerals, including coal and most other mined products—even to such "minerals" as sand, gravel, and oyster shells. More than half of the $2 billion of tax saving accrues to oil production, however.

These provisions have made the oil industry particularly attractive for investment by people in high personal income tax brackets. For example, a movie star who sees himself about to land in the 70 percent bracket can take part of his income and invest it in oil wells. If he strikes oil, the resultant income is taxable at a low rate because of the depletion allowance. If he misses a strike, he has only lost 30-cent dollars; the government would have received the other 70 cents anyway.

The depletion allowance has produced a distortion in investment decisions. Too much capital is attracted to the oil industry. As a result, the rate of return on oil has been driven down to the point where the after-tax return is little higher than the economy average. There is also much excess capacity.

In recent years, the depletion allowance has been justified in terms of the riskiness of this form of investment. Only one well drilled out of nine exploratory attempts produces enough oil to make it worth developing, though more than half of all production wells prove successful. The favorable tax treatment, it has been argued, is necessary to encourage people to enter this risky field.

Other companies also enjoy partial or complete exemption from the corporate income tax. Life insurance companies receive a different tax treatment because of the difficulty in defining their income, given the necessity of setting aside actuarial reserves against future claims. Commercial banks receive preferential tax treatment because they are allowed to set aside rather generous reserves against bad loans. Cooperatives, savings and loan associations, and mutual savings banks receive special treatment because they are not corporations in a legal sense and have some of the characteristics of nonprofit institutions. Where they compete with enterprises organized as corporations, they have a great advantage: they can undersell those who pay the full tax, and in some cases, have driven them out of business.

THE DOUBLE TAXATION ISSUE

It has been argued that it is unfair to levy both a personal and a corporation income tax, because it means that the same income is taxed twice. Suppose that a corporation produces an income of a million dollars. It will pay a corporation income tax of about one-half. Suppose that it pays the remaining half million dollars to its stockholders and that they pay an average tax rate of 60 percent on these dividends. Taking both taxes together, this means that out of the million dollars of income, the government collects a total of $800,000, leaving only $200,000 to the stockholders. If the money were earned by a part-

65

nership, the corporation income tax would not be paid at all; 48 percent seems a stiff price to pay for the privilege of incorporating.

In 1954, steps were taken to give relief by enacting a dividend exclusion and a dividend credit. The exclusion permitted every taxpayer to exclude the first $50 of dividends from his taxable income (the figure has since been raised to $100); the credit permitted him to deduct 4 percent of his dividends from his tax liability. The theory was that the corporation income tax is a form of withholding of the personal income tax on dividend income. A lower rate should then be applied in computing the personal tax.

These measures were thought to be first steps toward a more complete integration of the corporation and personal taxes into one comprehensive income tax. One might have envisaged that ultimately the entire corporation income tax on distributed profits would be considered withholding on the personal tax (which would entitle some people to refunds). A tax would still have to be levied on the part of profits retained by the corporation to keep the retained earnings from escaping taxation altogether. However, no further steps were taken, and Congress repealed the dividend credit in 1964.

Why has the double taxation theory not carried the day? First, the corporation income tax is probably shifted in part. To the extent that it is, one cannot speak of double taxation of stockholders because the burden is borne by consumers. Second, the corporation income tax can be considered a "doing business tax"—that is, a tax based on the benefit principle, a payment for the privilege of operating an enterprise within the framework of our economy. On that theory, all businesses, including partnerships and cooperatives, would be proper subjects of the tax; in fact, the government has attempted in recent years to tax more heavily some of the larger noncorporate enterprises, such as savings and loan associations, life insurance companies, and cooperatives, even if they do not adopt the conventional corporate form of organization. Third, are the corporation and its stockholders really synonymous? The double taxation theory views the corporation as no more than a legal intermediary between the stockholder and the income-creating production process. If the corporation is considered an independent institution, with its own purposes and motivations, then it may be an entity properly subject to taxation. Finally, and this may be the most important reason for the continued use of the corporation income tax, it is an excellent revenue raiser. Implicit in any scheme to lighten the total tax load so drastically is the necessity to find revenue substitutes, and it is hard to think of alternatives that would produce the $50 billion that we collect from this source.

TOWARD A MORE EQUAL DISTRIBUTION OF INCOME: A NEGATIVE INCOME TAX?

The tax system is a very powerful device for creating a more equal distribution of income. The progressive personal tax, even with its erosions, does tax the rich very substantially. The estate and gift taxes at least chip away at the concentration of wealth. The corporation income tax reduces the flow of re-investable financial resources of corporations, and this at least somewhat reduces their economic power.

But the tax system has only been used to reduce incomes, not to raise them. We have left the policies to raise incomes of the poor to the expenditure side of government budget. Could the tax system be used to give income rather than to take it away? Could the same, impersonal mechanisms that now determine tax payments according to one's income and family size be used to determine government disbursements to people with low incomes? Could we have a Negative Income Tax?

This powerful idea may become a reality in the United States. President Nixon's proposal, the Family Assistance Program, is designed to reform the welfare system by applying the logic and mechanisms of the tax system to help low income families. Coverage is still incomplete, benefits quite limited, and administration not yet as simple as in the positive tax system. But it is a large, first step and may be followed by others.

The conceptual structure of a negative income tax system is simple. The government: (1) defines a poverty income standard for families of different size, (2) makes negative income tax disbursements to bring the incomes of all families up to the standard, or at least to close a large fraction of their "poverty income gap."

The government has defined *poverty* in simple terms: a family is in poverty if its income is insufficient to achieve a certain (still very low) standard of living. If it does not receive such an income from its earnings or from the present programs of transfer payments, it should receive a "negative income tax" payment to bring it up to that level. A negative income tax would, in effect, provide a guaranteed minimum income. For example, the poverty standard for a family of four is about $4,000. If such a family had an income of $2,000 from other sources, a 100 percent negative income tax plan would pay it $2,000. A family with no income would receive the full poverty gap, or $4,000. The poverty standard for a single person is about $2,000; for a couple, $2,500; for a family of six it is $6,000. So, the payments would be large, and the initial direct cost of such a plan applicable to all the poor in this country would exceed $15 billion, or one-eighth of the positive income tax revenues.

A negative income tax plan that closed the poverty gap completely would seriously weaken work incentives. Many an unskilled worker supporting a family receives no more than the $4,000 of the poverty standard for a family of four. If he could receive the same income without working, why should he hold a job? Any earnings he would make would lose him an equal amount of negative tax payment; thus, in effect, he would confront a tax system in which the marginal rates are 100 percent. As people work less, the money cost of the negative income tax increases and the society loses real output. For this reason, a 100 percent plan is not feasible.

More modest negative income tax plans would not have as severe disincentives. For example, the plan could close 50 percent of the poverty gap (Fig.

67

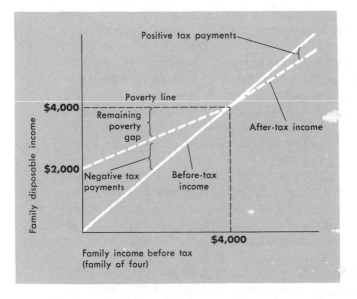

Positive tax payments

Poverty line

$4,000

Remaining poverty gap

After-tax income

$2,000

Negative tax payments

Before-tax income

Family disposable income

$4,000

Family income before tax
(family of four)

FIG. 5–3 A negative income tax plan.

5–3), thereby preserving an incentive to work, while still alleviating much of the poverty that remains in this country. Such a plan would cost about $8 billion.

Of course, we have several income maintenance programs already, including public assistance. But of the 30 million poor people in the United States, about half receive no help from any of the present programs. The unaided are mainly the working poor who work at very low wages or work irregularly and those eligible families who under the present programs have not applied because of ignorance or the indignity of going on welfare.

A negative income tax plan would be free of many of the faults of the present relief programs. There would be no degrading means tests, no repeated investigations to make sure that the family remains destitute. All the poor would receive a certain minimum of help, regardless of their location; today, rich states are usually generous to the poor; states with lesser resources provide far less assistance. And although the overall strategy against poverty must stress human investment to equip people to earn the income that lifts them out of poverty, there will inevitably be many families, particularly those without a potential breadwinner, for whom the human investment approach is not a realistic alternative.

PAYROLL TAXES

While the society experiments with negative income taxes to provide income supplements to the working poor, their positive tax burden has risen sharply in recent years. Apart from their share of sales and property taxes, the working poor pay taxes on their wages for social security and medicare. These payroll taxes now exceed 5 percent and are scheduled to go higher. Of course, they are also paid by middle income workers, with all wages up to a ceiling of $12,000 taxable. Because of this ceiling, these taxes are regressive. Employers pay matching amounts, some of which are probably shifted into lower wages and higher prices.

The rationale for this tax is the benefit principle. Social security and medicare are considered a form of insurance, for which eligibility depends on individual contributions. The self-financing character of these social insurance systems has made them popular and allowed them to grow. They are the most effective antipoverty programs that the United States has developed.

This benefit rationale is coming under increasing criticism as the burden on the poor rises and the share of total federal revenues coming from this source rises. In 1950, payroll taxes contributed 12 percent of all federal revenues; by 1960 the share had risen to 18 percent; in 1972, 29 percent of all federal revenues were payroll taxes.

The payroll taxes could be made less regressive through an exemption. If the first $1000 of wage income were not taxed, all contributors would pay less, but the percentage saving would be greater for the poor. An increase of the ceiling would also redistribute this tax burden, and it is planned to escalate the ceiling automatically in the future.

DISTRIBUTION OF THE TAX BURDEN
AND TRANSFER BENEFITS

Given the uncertainties of assigning the incidence of taxes and of estimating their economic effects, it is clearly impossible to discover the true distribution of the burden of taxation. Benefits of expenditures also need to be considered. The braver of public finance scholars have made elaborate calculations, using explicit assumptions on incidence. The most recent study, by Herriot and Miller, analyzes the tax burden for 1968. Table 5–2 summarizes their results. It also shows the distribution of transfer payments such as social security, medicare, welfare and unemployment insurance but does not allocate the benefits of defense, education, or other exhaustive expenditures.

Notice some of the findings:

1. The total tax burden is heaviest at the two ends of the income scale. Most income brackets pay about 30 percent of their income in taxes.

2. The poor pay heavy property taxes (for example, the retired person who owns his home) and a lot of sales and social security taxes. Indirectly, they pay some of the corporation income taxes through higher prices. The poor do receive $2 of transfers for every $1 of tax.

3. The rich pay relatively more federal income tax—that tax is genuinely progressive. (Their state income taxes and estate taxes are not shown separately.) The remaining burden on the rich is the corporate income tax that Herriot and Miller assume to be two-thirds borne by stockholders, one-third by consumers. (The studies cited on page 57 assumed more of this tax to be shifted.)

4. State and local taxes as a whole are very regressive because of their

69

Table 5–2 GOVERNMENT TAX AND TRANSFER RATES AS A PERCENTAGE OF TOTAL INCOME: 1968

Adjusted Money Income Levels	Total			Federal Taxes				State & Local Taxes		
	Taxes	Gov't Transfer Payments	Taxes Minus Transfer Payments	Total	Income Tax	Corp. Profit Tax	Social Security Tax	Total	Property Tax	Sales Tax
Tax & Transfer Rates—Total	31.6	6.9	24.6	21.7	9.5	4.7	5.1	9.9	3.7	2.8
Under $2,000	50.0	106.5	−56.5	22.7	1.2	6.0	7.6	27.2	16.2	6.6
$ 2,000 - $ 4,000	34.6	48.5	−13.9	18.7	3.5	4.6	8.5	15.7	7.5	4.9
$ 4,000 - $ 6,000	31.0	19.6	11.4	19.0	5.3	3.6	6.7	12.1	4.8	4.1
$ 6,000 - $ 8,000	30.1	8.6	21.5	19.4	6.5	3.2	6.8	10.7	3.8	3.6
$ 8,000 - $10,000	29.2	5.5	23.7	19.1	7.4	2.9	6.2	10.1	3.6	3.3
$10,000 - $15,000	29.8	3.9	25.9	19.9	8.7	2.9	5.8	9.9	3.6	2.9
$15,000 - $25,000	30.0	3.0	27.0	20.7	9.9	3.9	4.6	9.4	3.6	2.4
$25,000 - $50,000	32.8	2.1	30.7	25.0	12.9	7.5	2.5	7.8	2.7	1.8
$50,000+	45.0	0.4	44.7	38.4	19.8	15.4	1.0	6.7	2.0	1.1

Source: Roger A Herriot and Herman P. Miller, "The Taxes We Pay," The Conference Board Record, May 1971, p. 40.

reliance on property and sales taxes. If the tax-transfer system is the full measure of our egalitarian ideals, our eagerness to redistribute income is distinctly limited!

SUMMARY

The American tax system succeeds in raising an enormous amount of money to finance the government's activities at home and abroad. A tax system of such magnitude must be designed to minimize any negative impact on the performance of the economy.

The incidence of a tax does not always fall on the individuals on whom it is levied. Under some conditions, a tax can be shifted to someone else.

A good tax system must have certain administrative qualities, including certainty, low compliance and collection costs, enforceability, and acceptability.

The system must also be fair, both to promote the objective of an equitable distribution of income and to assure continued voluntary compliance by taxpayers. Two principles of equity have been advanced—the benefit principle, which has only limited applicability, and the ability-to-pay principle. Under the benefit principle, taxes are levied according to the benefit people receive from the expenditures for which the taxes are spent. Ability-to-pay involves questions of horizontal equity, of treating equals equally; and of vertical equity, the distribution of tax burdens among people with different abilities-to-pay.

Income is most commonly considered the best measure of ability-to-pay, although wealth and consumption expenditures have also been discussed. Taxes can be regressive, proportionate, or progressive, depending upon their relative burden on different income classes. Many of the issues of fairness relate to the federal personal income tax, our major policy instrument for changing the distribution of income. These issues relate to the use of the various exclusions, exemptions, and deductions under the tax. Their wide use under various special provisions of the tax law has led to an erosion of the tax base, with less than half of all personal income proving to be taxable. This erosion has led to higher tax rates to meet the financial needs of the government.

Other issues of fairness relate to the rather ineffective estate and gift taxes, and to the especially favorable treatment given to some industries and some forms of business organization under the corporation income tax. It has also been questioned whether it is fair to tax income from corporate business "twice," first as corporation income and then once more as individual dividend income.

In order to make the tax system an even more powerful instrument to promote a fair distribution of income, proposals for "negative income taxes" have been advanced. Such a plan could reduce the poverty income gap substantially, and would help the working poor particularly. Payroll taxes for social security and medicare are an important regressive element in the tax structure. They are contributing a rising share of all federal revenues. They could be made less regressive if an exemption were introduced.

Taxes,

Efficiency, and Growth

CHAPTER SIX

The preceding chapter dealt with the achievement of a fair tax system. This chapter discusses the effects of the tax system on two other long-term objectives, efficiency and growth. In the next chapter, we turn to the short-term objective of economic stability.

THE TAX SYSTEM
AND THE EFFICIENCY OF THE ECONOMY

Neutrality has long been considered one of the virtues of a good tax system. By this we mean that private production and consumption decisions are not affected, that the allocation of resources in the private sector remains undisturbed.

A tax system as pervasive as ours cannot be neutral. People do consider taxes in their personal and business decisions. An employee may decide not to bother with overtime because income taxes will take a quarter of the additional pay; a businessman may pass up the opportunity to make an investment because the prospective return after taxes is not worth the risk; a housewife may buy commodity B rather than A because A is subject to an excise tax and B is not. Perhaps someone may even smoke or drink a little less just because of the very high taxes on tobacco and alcohol.

Sometimes, the government favors a departure from neutrality, as in the case of liquor and tobacco. But usually, the influence on decision making is incidental to the government's need to raise revenue. The resultant departures from neutrality must be considered distortions in decision making.

These distortions are a serious matter in a market economy. We rely on consumers' expression of their preferences in the market to influence businesses in their production decisions. To show how taxes can distort this market mechanism, here is a simple example:

Suppose that consumers have been buying certain quantities of commodities A and B and that the price of A is \$3 and the price of B is \$3; these are equilibrium prices that reflect the relative attractiveness of the two commodities to consumers and the relative costs to producers. Now, suppose a tax of 30 cents is placed on A, and the price, including tax, goes up to \$3.20, the producers absorbing the remaining 10 cents of the tax. Consumers will normally buy less of A because it is priced higher in relation to B than before. Producers will also change their output; the price that they receive for A is now only \$2.90. Because of the tax, less of A is produced relative to B.

Assuming fully employed resources, the total goods available to the private economy have to fall if the government spends the tax revenues to purchase resources for its own use. This is unavoidable because the tax system is imposed to release the resources to be absorbed by the public sector. But in the example, there is an additional loss to the private economy. The price of A is no longer a sound signaling device that businesses can use to find out the value of A to consumers. The two sides of the market no longer operate by the same price. Consumers consider the price with tax, producers the price without tax. The tax has driven a wedge into the price system. As a result, the private economy is misled into producing the wrong combination of goods, underproducing those heavily taxed. Thus, the resources are no longer used in an optimal way. This additional loss, beyond the value of resources withdrawn from private use through the tax, is called the *dead-weight loss of taxation* because this loss has no offsetting gain to the government. It is simply the loss suffered from the reduction in the efficiency of the economy, a cost of having an imperfect tax system.

This argument is illustrated in Fig. 6–1. Suppose there are two commodities produced in the economy, B and A. The line F_0G_0 shows the production possibility curve for these two commodities. The other lines, such as i_0, show the community's indifference curves, obtained by combining the indifference curves of individual consumers. In equilibrium, and without a tax, the economy will produce b_0 of B and a_0 of A. At that production point, the marginal rates of substitution of consumers are equal to the slope of the production possibility curve; that is, they are equal to the ratios of the marginal costs of B and A. The allocation of resources is efficient; the level of welfare corresponds to the indifference curve i_0.

Now suppose the government can raise money through a neutral tax, one that has no effects except to withdraw resources from private uses. By cutting private purchasing power, such a tax leaves some resources free for government use. The government obtains these resources by spending the tax proceeds. Figure 6–2 shows this case. The new production possibility curve for the private economy, F_1G_1, is inside the previous one, linking only smaller possible combinations of producing A and B.

73

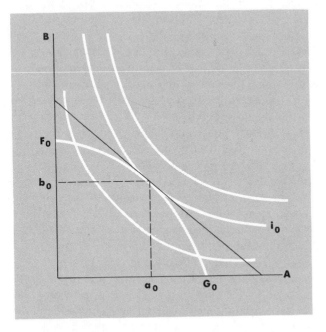

FIG. 6–1 Resource allocation before tax distortion.

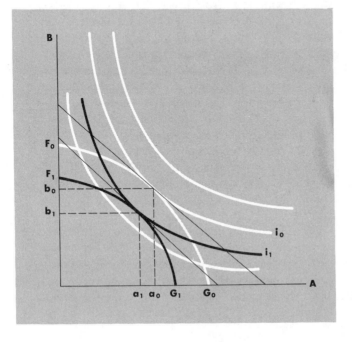

FIG. 6–2 Effect of a tax without distortion of resource allocation.

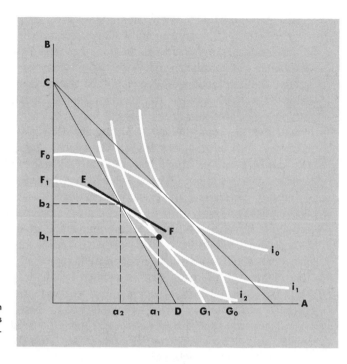

FIG. 6–3 Resource allocation after tax distortion. The excess burden of taxation is the difference between i_1 and i_2.

But because the neutral tax does not affect decisions, resource allocation remains efficient. A new price line is tangent both to the new production possibility curve and to a (lower) community indifference curve. Prices still do their job, bringing marginal rates of substitution and relative marginal costs to equality. The efficient combination of A and B is a_1 and b_1.

Now, suppose that the government wishes to withdraw resources from private uses by imposing an excise tax on commodity A (Fig. 6–3). The production possibility curve for the private sector is again reduced to F_1G_1, because fewer resources are left for private production. There are now two price lines: the consumers face the price line CD; they pay a higher price for A than the producers receive. The price line for producers is EF. At the equilibrium point, the community's indifference curve will be tangent to CD at the point a_2b_2. At that point, then marginal rate of substitution equals the before-tax relative price, reflected in the slope of CD. The consumers reach a level of welfare represented by the indifference curve i_2. The producers manufacture the combination a_2b_2 for which the marginal costs are in the same ratio as the relative prices after tax as reflected by the slope of the line EF.

The new solution is an equilibrium: the amounts produced equal the amounts consumed, a_2 of A and b_2 of B and all resources are fully employed. Consumers cannot improve their welfare at the given prices; producers cannot raise their profits by changing the combination of outputs. However, it is not the right equilibrium. At a_2b_2, the community is on the indifference curve i_2, which is inferior to i_1. The consumers would prefer a_1b_1 over a_2b_2, and the resources could produce the better combination. But the distortions in the decisions of consumers and producers result in the selection of the wrong combination of goods. The difference in welfare between the indifference curves i_1 and i_2 is the dead-weight tax loss; it is the excess burden of taxation attributable to the distortion in resource allocation.

From the point of view of having an efficient allocation of resources in the economy, it is desirable to have a tax system that causes as little dead-weight tax loss as possible. This is accomplished by levying taxes in such a way that decision making is not affected—that is to say, that the tax cannot be avoided by adjusting behavior. The extreme form of such a tax is a head tax, a lump-sum tax imposed on living persons. It cannot be avoided, and hence does not change economic behavior. But because the amount to be paid has to be the same for everybody, it has to be set low so that it can be borne by low-income people; hence not much money can be raised by this method. No other tax is completely unavoidable. Excise taxes can be avoided by buying less of the taxed commodities; income taxes can be avoided by working less and earning less income; property taxes can be avoided by holding less property, and so on.

There are two general rules for keeping the dead-weight loss at a minimum while raising any given amount of revenue. First, only those things should be taxed that generate slight adjustments in behavior. In the case of excise taxation, this means that more revenue should be raised from those items for which the demand and supply are inelastic. Governments discovered early that commodities with inelastic demands could be taxed successfully. In the Middle Ages, the salt tax was used widely. People needed salt for their diet; there was no substitute. Hence, salt had an inelastic demand. Today, gasoline, liquor, and tobacco seem to play the same role. Unfortunately, the principle of minimizing dead-weight tax loss runs counter to the equity objective. Items in inelastic demand tend to be necessities, like salt and bread, that take a larger fraction of the budgets of low-income families.

The second rule for minimizing the dead-weight tax loss is to maintain high average rates of taxation with low marginal rates. The dead-weight tax loss originates in the induced changes of private decisions at the margin, and hence depends on the marginal tax rates. On the other hand, average rates determine the total revenue. Thus, a tax causes less dead-weight tax loss per dollar of revenue if its average rate is high but the marginal rate is low. Many of our taxes, such as excise taxes and most property taxes, are proportionate, making marginal and average rates the same. But our personal income tax has the opposite characteristic, with marginal rates higher than average rates, so the incentive to change decisions is strong in relation to the total revenue that is raised. The conflict between meeting the goals of equity and efficiency is particularly clear in this case.

PROGRESSIVE INCOME TAXES
AND THE SUPPLY OF EFFORT

The single most important question about the effect of the U.S. income tax system on the economy's efficiency is the impact of the high marginal tax rates on people's willingness to put forth their best productive efforts. If a man has to pay in taxes, say, one-half of his income from extra work—perhaps a lawyer working weekends, a doctor taking on additional patients, or a salesman making evening calls—his incentive will certainly be reduced. No one can doubt that these effects are pertinent. The question is: How widespread and how important are they? For if the high rates have diminished effort substantially throughout the economy, we are giving up a lot of economic performance for the sake of equity.

Three major studies have been conducted on this question. The classic study is by Professor Sanders of the Harvard Business School, who interviewed 160 corporate executives.[1] He found that the typical executive has to put forth his best efforts, taxes or no, to fulfill the requirements of his job and to progress on the promotional ladder of his company. Further, executives are not motivated by income alone; equally important is the desire to do a good job, to be favorably recognized by fellow executives, and to know the excitement that comes from conducting a business successfully. Although salary is very important as an indicator of the place of the executive in the hierarchy of the company and as a symbol of achievement, it is the relative salary compared to others that is important in this regard. Because everyone pays taxes, the symbolic value of salary is undiminished. Furthermore, the companies adapt their method of payment to executives to reduce tax liability, through stock options, pension plans, and other devices.

But in certain areas, the negative effect of the tax system was very clear. The willingness of executives to move from one company to another, or from one location to another is definitely reduced, and this is especially true of older upper-level executives. Typically, they have sizable stakes in the pension plans of their present company that they would forfeit if they were to resign; it would be very difficult for another company to match these accumulated pension rights. In the case of locational changes, a middle-aged family will have taken root in the community, have friends and a home to which they have become accustomed. To pull up stakes at this stage in life imposes psychic costs for which no moving allowance can compensate, yet the resultant increase in after-tax income may not be very great because of the progressive tax. The number of people in

---

[1] T. H. Sanders, *Effects of Taxation on Executives*, Harvard Graduate School of Business Administration, Division of Research, 1951.

this position, upper-level executives asked to change jobs or locations, is not great, but they are important. Our capitalist economy depends on the skill of top management. Competition for the top positions and for the top personnel—even across company lines—is necessary to put the right man into the right post. The tax system has clearly made this more difficult.

Professor Break of the University of California at Berkeley interviewed 306 lawyers and accountants in England.[2] This was an ideal group to study because top-income tax rates are even higher in England than in this country, and lawyers and accountants are independent professional men who control their own work effort; they can take on fewer clients, take longer vacations, or retire earlier. Break found that the men interviewed fell into three groups. Forty men reported that taxes had a definite adverse effect on incentive, ranging from blanket refusal to accept additional work, to reduced effort in seeking new clients, to occasionally turning down unattractive work. Thirty-one men complained that they had to work harder because of taxes. Some of them said that they were unable to retire when they wished because they had been unable to accumulate sufficient wealth. Others reported that they had to work harder day-by-day in order to realize an after-tax income sufficient to sustain the standard of living to which they were accustomed. The remaining 235 men reported minor or no effects on their work, although many grumbled quite a bit about taxes. Typically, they enjoyed their work, were happy to have a large and successful practice, and felt they owed it to their clients to do the best for them they could.

A third study was conducted by the Survey Research Center of the University of Michigan. This group interviewed 957 individuals with incomes of at least $10,000 a year, some with very high incomes.[3] They found that, despite the high tax rates, their median work week was 48 hours with one out of four working 60 hours. One out of eight individuals indicated that they worked less because of taxes. The reduction of work effort was most common in the $40 to $90,000 income brackets, where one out of five said they worked less.

These studies deal only with very specialized groups of people. What about the general working population? Our evidence is extremely limited, but so far nothing suggests that unions have insisted on a shorter work week, that workers have refused to work overtime, or that fewer wives enter the labor force because of taxes.[4]

In summary, then, it appears that the adverse effect of personal income taxes on the supply of effort is probably slight. This is because people are not motivated by money income alone because the extent of their control over their

[2] G. F. Break, "Income Taxes and Incentives to Work: an Empirical Study," *American Economic Review*, Vol. XLVII, No. 5, September 1957, pp. 529–49.

[3] R. Barlow, H. E. Brazer, and J. N. Morgan, *Economic Behavior of the Affluent* (Washington, D. C.: The Brookings Institution, 1966), pp. 138–39.

[4] In England, however, where there is no income-splitting (the wife's income is added to the husband's and the total is taxed at one progressive rate schedule), the tax system raises greater obstacles to women joining the labor force.

own working conditions is limited and because the methods of payment by employers have been adapted to reduce the tax burden.

This brings us to what is perhaps the most important distortion caused by the tax system in our economy: the social waste of tax avoidance itself. According to our principles of law, a person has no obligation to pay more taxes than is legally required. The tax law clearly presents to all upper- and many middle-income taxpayers the opportunity to reduce their tax burden significantly by rearranging their personal affairs. Seeking out capital gains rather than ordinary income on investments, organizing personal wealth into trusts, buying tax-exempt local bonds, taking income in the form of pensions, stock options, or deferred compensation contracts—these are all legal and reputable means of avoiding taxes. As we have lived with our present tax system, people have learned to use these devices. Consequently, an immense amount of effort has gone into tax avoidance. Corporation executives who should be spending all their time thinking about the affairs of their companies are distracted into managing their personal investments so they will yield capital gains or other tax advantages. Family financial arrangements are set up not only from a personal but also from a tax point of view. For example, income and estate taxes are reduced if wealth is not left to children but is put in trust for a later generation, with only the income accruing to the children; as a result, the second generation never acquires the maturing responsibility of managing the family wealth. The job is turned over to professional trustees, banks, and lawyers, who manage the wealth conservatively and do not make the funds available for risky ventures.

The tax system has also created a profession of experts, of accountants and lawyers who advise people on their tax affairs. If our tax system were simpler, with lower rates and fewer loopholes, the keen intellectual qualities of this group could be devoted to other purposes. And increasing tax-avoidance constitutes a threat to the tax system itself. As taxpayer morale weakens, the tax base erodes, and tax rates need to be kept high to produce necessary revenues.

THE CORPORATION INCOME TAX
AND ECONOMIC DEVELOPMENT

As economic development became a recognized national goal, the question was raised more and more insistently whether the tax system had a retarding effect. Several major tax changes have already been made to facilitate growth and development and others are under consideration. The re-examination continues, and several far-reaching proposals are being debated.

Because the United States relies so heavily on corporations for her industrial capital formation, it is the corporation income tax that has to be given particular attention in dealing with the issue of taxation and growth. The tax affects (1) the incentive to invest—that is, the profit anticipated from an invest-

79

ment; (2) the riskiness of investment; and (3) the volume of business saving and hence the supply of investible funds.

The structure of the tax is simple. Its base is the net income or profit of the corporation. The basic rate is a flat 48 percent, except for the first $25,000 of income on which the rate is 22 percent. There is no exemption.

The incidence of the corporation income tax has not been isolated with certainty or precision. When first imposed, a large part of the tax is likely to fall on the taxed companies. But as time passes, shifting can occur in several ways: after-tax profits may be partially restored as firms raise prices; the oligopolistic firm may have after-tax profit targets that it will try to reach through higher prices if the government raises the tax share of profits. In competitive industries, the tax will reduce the supply of funds, and over a period of years, will affect the total capital stock. A lower capital stock means that capital is a relatively more scarce factor of production in the firm—and this, in turn, may mean that its rate of return is greater. Thus, the slower growth of capital, other things being kept the same, may gradually offset the tax and restore the return per unit of capital. It is less likely to restore the total after-tax profit because there will be fewer units of capital earning the return.

To the extent the tax is not shifted, it makes the government a partner in every corporation, taking half of all profits. Investment projects will be undertaken only if their expected return exceeds the cost of capital and compensates for the risk being taken. Inevitably, companies will invest less if the government receives half the gain.

There are some qualifications to this picture. First, while the government is a partner in the gains, to some extent it also is a partner in the losses. When a project turns out badly, the company is permitted to subtract the loss from the profits it earns elsewhere, thus reducing its tax by one-half of the losses. Where a company has no profits from other activities against which to offset losses, it is free to "carry" the losses "forward" against the profits of the five following years, or it can carry them "backward" against profits in the three preceding years. These loss offsets are incomplete (1) because some companies never have any profits against which to offset losses, and (2) even if a project has failed, some of the losses cannot be written off until the fixed capital depreciates, and this may mean a delay in the tax-saving of many years. Thus, although our tax system makes provision for comparable treatment of gains and losses, the symmetry is less than complete, and to some extent the tax does have the effect of making investment a "Tails you win, heads I lose" proposition.

The Corporation Income Tax and the Supply of Investible Funds

The tax is also important because it affects the internal supply of a company's capital. Most industrial corporations rely chiefly on internally raised capital for their expansion. They are reluctant to borrow money or to sell additional stock because the cost may be high, and the outsiders who supply the capital may limit the future actions of management. Corporations are usually anxious to reinvest the capital they generate internally—the depreciation allowances and retained profits—but will go outside the company for capital only when the investment opportunities are really attractive or exceptionally necessary for the business to preserve its market role. The corporation income tax takes away a share of the internal funds, the kind of capital most likely to be reinvested.

This effect of the tax on the supply of funds is particularly important for new and growing enterprises. It is especially difficult for them to raise outside capital because they are not well-known and are regarded as particularly risky. If a relatively new company has developed a new product, it must expand rapidly if it is to succeed; otherwise older companies will imitate its product and take over the market. By absorbing up to half of all the profits, the tax greatly reduces the rate of expansion possible from internal capital. To illustrate, suppose a new company with a successful product earns 40 percent on its capital and suppose that it starts with an investment of $100,000. It earns $40,000 the first year, which it reinvests; it earns $56,000 the second year, $78,000 the third year, and so on. By the end of the seventh year, the company would have total capital of $1,053,000. With a tax of 50 percent, the first year's profits would be only $20,000, the second year's, $24,000, the third year's, $29,000, and so on. And if all of it is again reinvested, the value at the end of the seventh year would be $358,000. The tax prevents the kind of rapid build-up of capital that a new, expanding company requires.

As a result of this difficulty under the present corporation income tax, as well as other tax factors,[5] many small, growing firms sell out to large established companies and disappear. This is a serious matter for the economy because we depend on the rise of new companies to keep the old giants on their toes and to keep the top corporate ranks open.

The Tax Treatment of Depreciation

One of the costs subtracted from gross revenue before computing income is depreciation, the cost of the deterioration of physical capital. If depreciation accounting is skipped, as was widely practiced before 1920, income will be overstated because, sooner or later, the equipment or the building will lose its usefulness and value. Depreciation accounting tries to solve the problem of allocating

---

[5] Personal income and estate taxes also push small companies into mergers. If a successful entrepreneur were to draw income from his business, he would have to pay the high personal rates. The only way he can withdraw his wealth from the business without paying the personal tax is by selling the business and reaping a capital gain, which will then be taxed at a more favorable rate.

To pay estate taxes, a business must be liquid, but a growing company keeps its capital in equipment, inventories, and buildings, not in cash. All too frequently, the founder of the business anticipates this difficulty by merging with a larger company in exchange for stock that is marketable. (The government has attempted to give some relief to this problem by letting an estate pay the duty on a business over a 10-year period.)

the cost of durable capital items to specific years, so that net income, after allowing for capital deterioration, can be properly identified.

The measurement of depreciation is difficult. How much of a machine should be written off in the first year and how much in other years? An engineering approach that measures physical wear and increasing maintenance costs could be tried, but this overlooks economic obsolescence, the fact that better machines become available and that the demand for the product may disappear.

In the absence of a logical solution, simple rules of thumb have come into universal use. Most commonly, the historical cost of physical capital has been allocated in equal amounts to each year of its economic life, so that the value of an item, as recorded on the balance sheet, declines by the same amount each year. This procedure is called the *straightline method* of depreciation.

In recent decades, businessmen became dissatisfied with this method as they discovered that the economic value of machines declined faster than proportionately over time. In the used-equipment market, a one-year-old machine is worth much less than a new one; later on, value declines more slowly. Businessmen also found that for investment to be successful, they had to recoup a good part of their cost during the early years of economic life.

Depreciation accounting is especially important from the point of view of taxation. Because it is a deduction from corporate income, every dollar of extra depreciation represents a tax saving of 48 cents. If the depreciation method allowed by the tax authorities is too slow, the government is taxing more than the actual income of the business; or to put it in another way, the government takes its share of profits earlier than they are really earned. Because most firms are heavily dependent on their internal supply of funds for investment, this is a serious matter in terms of company growth. It becomes especially acute in a period of inflation, when even the best depreciation method based on historical cost does not provide sufficient funds to replace the equipment at its now inflated price.

For these reasons, the government encouraged the use of two more liberal standard depreciation methods in 1954. These are the *declining balance* and the *sum-of-the-years-digit* methods (see Fig. 6–4). But even the 1954 depreciation reforms did not prove adequate. The tax laws of our chief competitors abroad in Western Europe and Japan were more generous than our own, giving an advantage to their companies in the highly competitive international markets;[6] and so the United States took additional steps. Instead of fixing the economic life of thousands of individual items of equipment, a "guideline life" has been established for each industry that can be applied to all equipment. The guidelines permit short lives, allowing businesses to write off equipment quickly.

[6] France has developed the art of the tax treatment of depreciation to the highest point. Special treatment is accorded industries in which the government wants to invest heavily, such as export industries. Also, the capital has been multiplied by revaluation factors to offset the effects of past inflation.

METHOD	DEPRECIATION OF MACHINE WITH ECONOMIC LIFE OF FIVE YEARS				
	Year 1	Year 2	Year 3	Year 4	Year 5
Straightline	20%	20%	20%	20%	20%
Double declining balance	Double straightline 40%	2/5 of remaining balance 24%	2/5 of remaining balance 14.44%	2/5 of remaining balance 8.64%	2/5 of remaining balance 5.18%*
Sum-of-the-years digits	$\dfrac{5}{5+4+3+2+1}$ 33.33%	$\dfrac{4}{5+4+3+2+1}$ 26.67%	$\dfrac{3}{5+4+3+2+1}$ 20%	$\dfrac{2}{5+4+3+2+1}$ 13.33%	$\dfrac{1}{5+4+3+2+1}$ 6.67%

*Because the declining balance method never completes a write-off, the government allows a late switch to the straightline method.

FIG. 6–4 Three methods of depreciation: an example.

The Investment Credit

Eager to encourage investment, the United States adopted a new device in 1962. It permits firms to deduct each year from their tax liability 7 percent of their total current investment outlays on equipment. Thus, in effect, the government pays a subsidy on investments by giving back to firms a fraction of the investment cost through this special tax credit. This method is a particularly powerful incentive for stimulating growth per dollar of tax revenue lost. The tax relief directly benefits those firms most willing to invest.

The investment credit has been criticized on the grounds that it is a deliberate departure from tax neutrality. The tax system is being used to get businessmen to change their decisions, to undertake more investment than their ordinary judgment would dictate. Thus, this is a very explicit attempt by the government to interfere in the private economy in a manner designed to raise the rate of investment, and thereby the rate of growth and development.

THE TAX SYSTEM AND PERSONAL SAVING

Although business saving is the most important source of capital for industry, personal saving also makes a contribution. Rapidly growing enterprises

83

as well as public utilities with their enormous capital requirements must look outside their businesses, to the capital market, for both equity and debt capital. It is personal saving, the saving of households, that must provide the bulk of the long-term funds available in the capital market.

The marginal propensity to save is higher for families with larger incomes. In fact, as a whole, lower- and middle-income families do not save a great deal; furthermore, their savings tend to be channeled into home mortgages (through their banks and life insurance companies) or into government bonds. Thus, industry depends largely on the savings of a relatively small number of upper-income families. A strongly progressive income tax falls particularly heavy on this very group of people. Here, then, is another potential area in which the tax system could retard economic development.

Professors Butters, Thompson, and Bollinger of the Harvard Business School investigated whether the personal income tax had affected personal saving. They interviewed 750 active investors, most of them in the crucial high-income brackets. They found that the tax structure had "substantially reduced the capacity of upper bracket individuals to accumulate new investible funds, but that . . . their remaining capacity is still very large."[7] More importantly, the study found that the pattern of investment was very much affected, with most investors acknowledging that they had rearranged their investment behavior because of tax considerations. On the whole, the tax system tended to polarize investors into one of two types: (1) those who originally were income- and security-minded tended to buy tax-exempt bonds of state and local governments and life insurance policies, as the extra income to be gained from other securities was shrunk by taxes; (2) those investors who were appreciation-minded, on the other hand, were made more willing to take risks, and placed their capital into such ventures as speculative common stocks held for capital gains, real estate benefiting from liberal depreciation allowances, and oil properties receiving the depletion allowance.

Thus, the retarding effects on saving of the high progressive rates of the personal income tax are mitigated by the special tax treatment accorded some particular kinds of investments. The adjustments of investment behavior to the tax structure have continued to make venture capital available from personal saving. This is a crucial point for the growth of the economy. The private investor, however, is not free to consider all opportunities on their merit and then to choose those that he considers to be the most promising. Instead, he is pulled and pushed by the tax structure out of and into certain kinds of investments. And apart from the general departures from a rational allocation of personal investments, it has brought about some specific side-effects that have been a

[7] J. K. Butters, L. E. Thompson, and L. L. Bollinger, *Effects of Taxation on Investments by Individuals*, Harvard Graduate School of Business Administration, 1953, p. 29. See also R. Barlow, H. E. Brazer and J. Morgan, *Economic Behavior of the Affluent*, Brookings Institution, 1966, for similar findings.

mixed blessing. On the one hand, the inducement to buy tax-exempt state and local securities has provided a market for the great volume of bonds that states and localities have had to issue to finance their rising education and other costs. On the other hand, the preoccupation with capital gains rather than dividend income accentuates the speculative elements in the stock market.

TOO MUCH INCOME TAXATION?
THE VALUE-ADDED TAX AS AN ALTERNATIVE

Although no one piece of evidence or one line of argument clearly shows our personal and corporate income taxes to have really serious retarding effects on the performance of the economy, there is sufficient uneasiness about the issue to have led to a search for a major new source of revenue.

The value-added tax has been advanced as a substitute for all, or part, of the corporation income tax. France pioneered this tax, and the European Economic Community as a whole is adopting it as its major business tax. Its base is the "value added" of each business, defined as the total value of output minus the value of purchased material inputs; this is equal to profits plus interest plus depreciation plus payments to labor. Thus, the tax has a broader base than profits: it also taxes payrolls, depreciation, and interest. Levied only on corporations, it could raise as much money as our present corporate income tax with a rate only about one-third as high. It could also be applied to a wider range of businesses, including cooperatives and other unincorporated enterprises, thus making possible even lower rates through a broader base.

The tax has some theoretical advantages. It taxes all factors of production at the same rate unlike the corporation income tax, which is a tax on the return to capital only. Thus, it does not lead to distortions in business choices about the optimal combination of the factors of production. Whereas the corporation income tax leads to a less-than-optimal use of capital by taxing that factor and not others, the value-added tax is neutral in this regard. It would encourage the substitution of capital for labor, because it would ease the tax on capital and impose a tax on labor: labor-saving investments would be made more attractive because the cost of labor—and hence the gain from labor saving—would be raised by that part of the tax that falls on the company's wage payments. It would also be neutral between the various forms of business organization, taxing not only corporations. Finally, the tax could reach industries that enjoy favored treatment under the present tax, such as the oil industry.

On the other hand, the incidence of the tax differs from the corporate tax in a regressive manner. A change from one tax to the other would, in effect, be a partial change from a tax on profits to a tax on wages. Some of the incidence of the tax would fall on the workers. Furthermore, the tax would be more likely to be passed on in higher prices and hence be shifted to consumers. Finally—

85

and this is where the objectives of efficiency and equity clash most clearly—the value-added tax would fall relatively more heavily on unsuccessful companies and less on successful ones. Even a company that made little or no profit would have to pay the value-added tax and might even be put out of business by it, whereas the burden on successful, high-profit companies would be eased. From the point of view of having funds available for reinvestment in the expanding, high-profit sectors of the economy and withdrawing capital from declining sectors, the change would be desirable (though this line of argument does not apply to high profits based on monopoly rather than rising demands). But what about the social and human aspects of declining industries and depressed areas? Should the tax system be changed to make their problems more acute?[8]

THE TAX SYSTEM
AND THE GROWTH OF DEMAND

In the preceding section, we have discussed the relation of the tax system to the growth of the economy's capacity to produce. We assumed that more effort means more output, more saving leads to more investment and more productive capacity. Thus, we looked at growth only from the point of view of the potential supply of output. But to achieve growth, both supply and demand must grow at a proper rate. When demand grows too rapidly, inflation results. When demand is sluggish, unemployment and idle capacity develop. The tax system helps determine whether supply and demand grow in balance because it affects the rates of growth of both supply and demand.

As income grows, tax collections grow as well, reducing the growth of purchasing power and effective demand. Not all taxes respond in the same proportions. For example, a progressive income tax will rise faster than income because taxpayers enter higher brackets, so that not only the tax base but also the average effective tax rates increases. Gasoline, liquor, and tobacco excises rise much less than income because the amount of consumption of these items responds only mildly to income growth.

It would be sheer chance if the revenue response of the tax system to growth were precisely such as to keep the growth of supply and demand in balance. Corrective policies to maintain this balance—that is, to maintain full employment without excess demand, are the subject of Chapter Eight. Here, let us only keep in mind that measures designed to improve the structure of the tax system for the sake of growth of supply can be nullified if the aggregate response of tax collections to economic growth is too severe, keeping demand too low.

---

[8] The value-added tax has also been proposed as a substitute for the property taxes levied by local governments. To assure a more uniform tax base for financing education, the federal government would levy this new tax and distribute the proceeds to school districts in a form of revenue sharing.

SUMMARY

The tax system affects the efficiency of resource allocation within the economy. A selective system of excise taxes, for example, upsets the marginal conditions necessary for efficient resource allocation by confronting producers with a different set of relative prices from that faced by consumers. The personal income tax can affect the supply of labor, particularly of individuals paying high marginal rates. Empirical studies so far suggest that these effects are moderate. Executive mobility has, however, been impaired, and much effort is wasted on tax avoidance.

The tax system also affects the growth of the economy. The corporation income tax affects the incentive to invest and the supply of investible funds. Some important measures have been taken in recent years to ameliorate these effects, including liberalization of depreciation allowances and an investment credit.

Finally, the tax system can affect the amount of personal saving and investment. Its influence on the patterns of personal investment behavior is probably more important than its effects on total personal saving and investment.

Although no one single retarding effect has been discovered that would justify a drastic rearrangement of our tax system, there is some feeling that the federal government relies too heavily on income taxation. The value-added tax is the most commonly proposed alternative.

The Economics

of the Public Debt

CHAPTER SEVEN

When revenues fall short of expenditures, governments borrow. Over the years, this process has left most governments with large outstanding debts. In a sense, the national debt is the debt of all of us. And yet, we are not only the taxpayers but also the bond holders. Interest has to be paid on these debts by the taxpayers, and when the bonds expire, they have to be repaid or refinanced through new borrowing.

In this brief chapter, we consider the question: What is the burden of debt? It turns out to be a rather more intricate matter than appears at first glance.

GROWTH OF DEBT

Figure 7–1 shows the growth of the national public debt since World War I. About one-third of the $25 billion borrowed in World War I was repaid in the 1920s. The years of the Great Depression saw the debt increase from $16 billion to $40 billion. But most of the debt was acquired during World War II, at the end of which it had reached $259 billion. Thereafter, it stayed level until 1957, with surpluses occurring in some years of prosperity and deficits occurring in recession and in some of the Korean War years. Since 1957, the debt has increased, from $272 billion to $456 billion by 1972. The increase in the debt is largely due to war, and secondarily to periods of unemployment when the response to economic conditions—falling revenues and rising expenditures—has put the budget into deficit.

The figure $456 billion is high—$2,180 for every man, woman,

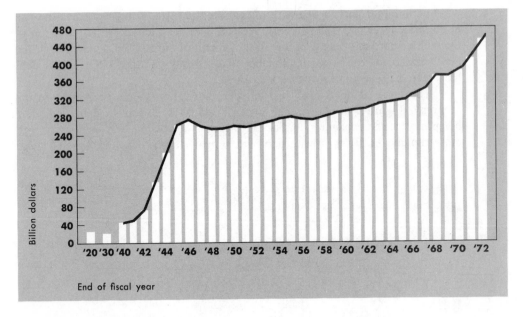

FIG. 7–1 The federal debt.

and child in the United States. But to interpret this figure, it must be put into some perspective. Figure 7–2 shows the ratio of the national debt to GNP, which, in a general way, is the tax base out of which the interest cost must be met. This ratio has fallen steadily since its World War II peak. In 1946, the debt was 130 percent of GNP; in 1972 it had fallen to 42 percent. This decline

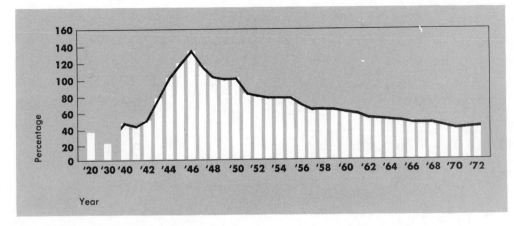

FIG. 7–2. Federal debt as a percentage of GNP.

was due in larger part to a growth of real output (up 150 percent) plus the rise in the price level (up 120 percent). We can take satisfaction in the reduction of the relative burden of the debt due to the growth of output; but the decline of the real burden caused by repeated inflations means only that the holders of the debt have seen the real value of their bonds eroded.

The national debt must also be seen in relation to the total debt in the economy. Figure 7–3 shows that since World War II private debt, including home mortgages, consumer credit, and business borrowing, has increased much more rapidly. In 1946, private debt was somewhat less than the national debt;

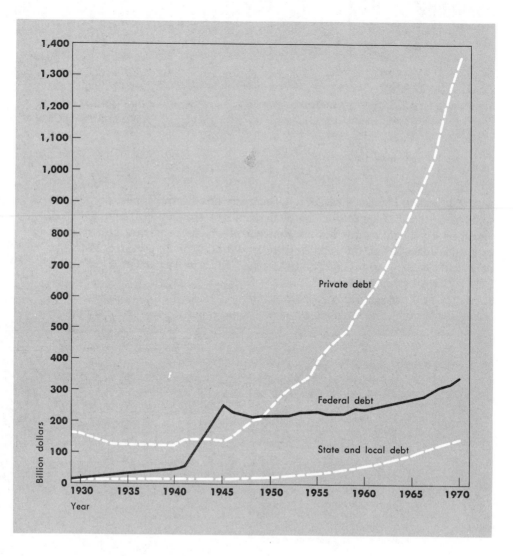

FIG. 7–3 National debt in relation to total debt.

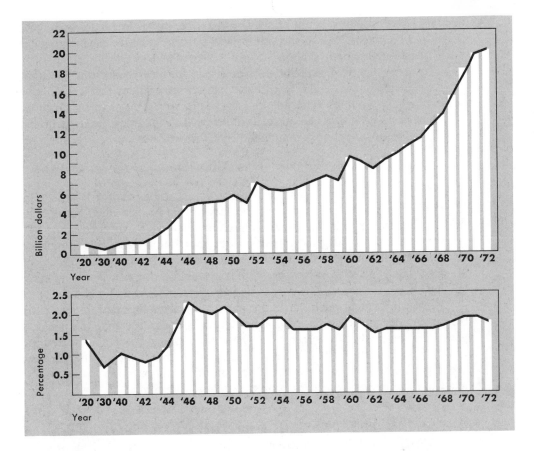

FIG. 7–4 Federal interest payments in billions of dollars and as a percentage of GNP.

by 1970 it was four times as great. In the public sector, state and local debt increased sharply.

Another relevant dimension of the debt is the volume of interest payments. This is a payment that has to be made by the taxpayers every year and depends not only on the size of the debt but also on the average interest rate. Figure 7–4 shows both the absolute interest payments on the national debt as well as their relationship to GNP. Interest payments have increased considerably more than the debt itself because rates have been on a rising trend through much of this period. As the older low-interest securities have had to be refinanced, the government has had to pay substantially higher interest rates.

WHAT IS THE BURDEN OF THE DEBT?

With a national debt of $2,180 per capita, it is only natural that it occupy the minds of politicians, editorial writers, citizens, and economists. Intuition tells us we would be better off without the debt, just as we would wish to be free of personal debts. Yet to sort out the real burdens from the fancied requires the most careful economic analysis.

To define the burden of the debt precisely, we have to ask this question: What difference does it make to us and to future generations that certain past government expenditures were financed by borrowing rather than by taxation? For if they had been financed out of taxation, there would now be no debt and there could be no "burden" of that debt.

The Burden in Terms of Real Resources

Two-thirds of our national debt was acquired during World War II. The tangible burden of that war certainly does not rest on our shoulders today. The lives lost and the material resources required to win it were expended in the war years; no financial arrangements can change that simple fact. Even though a large national debt was incurred in the years 1942 to 1945, future generations are not being asked to fight the war. Thus, the real cost of past war expenditures has already been incurred.

What about debt incurred during periods of unemployment? In this case, the real burden of deficit-financed expenditures is limited even at the time expenditures are made. Resources would have been idle, so no other outputs are foregone. In fact, output is likely to be increased by the multiplier effects of the initial spending. Thus, the creation of debt in this situation raises output and is likely to raise investment and the total growth of the economy.

External Versus Internal Debts

When an underdeveloped country borrows abroad to build a dam, or when a town issues bonds to build a new high school, it acquires an external debt that has to be repaid at some future date. Just as in the case of an individual, the borrowing increases the total resources available initially but reduces the resources available in the future. To meet the interest and repayment charges owed to the outside world, the government must reduce future public spending or raise taxes and thereby reduce future private spending. In each case, it cuts total internal resource use. In effect, the borrowing simply makes the resources available earlier in exchange for the commitment to pay interest. The initial increase in total available resources is made possible by borrowing done outside the community. Similarly, interest and repayment means that the community gives up resources to the outside world later on.

When our national government borrows, the process is not the same. The borrowing occurs within the country, so that the total resources available to the country as a whole are not increased. The resources are simply transferred from the bond-buyers to the government, which expends them for public purposes. Similarly, the interest and repayment charges do not transfer resources outside the country as a whole but only transfer them from the taxpayers to the bond-holders. This distinction between an external and an internal debt is funda-mental. An internally held debt represents only a commitment to effect a certain transfer of purchasing power among the individuals within the country. It does not commit the country to give up real output to another country.

Thus, when it comes to the national debt, there is a fundamental truth in the phrase, "We owe it to ourselves," although, as we shall see in a moment, "we" is not always the same individuals, and there are some harmful side effects that are a real burden.

Loss of Output: The Tax Costs
of Financing Interest Payments

One burden of a public debt is unambiguous. Extra taxes have to be im-posed to finance the interest payments. These taxes lead to some loss of real out-put because of their distorting and disincentive effects. Even though the redistri-bution of income from the taxpayers to the bond holders is only a transfer payment, it does contribute to the negative effects of the tax system that we dis-cussed at length in the preceding chapter. This dead-weight loss is borne year after year as the interest payments continue to be met. Had the debt not been incurred earlier, this loss would not be suffered; hence it is a genuine burden of the debt.[1]

Loss of Output: Reduced Investment?

Should debt financing of public spending lead to a decline in investment, there would be another unambiguous loss of output. Future generations would inherit a small stock of capital, an economy with a smaller capacity to produce, hence a smaller output. How could debt financing reduce private investment? First, under conditions of full employment and with an unchanged monetary policy, the government borrowing is competitive with private borrowing, interest rates will be raised by the deficit, and investment reduced. This is not the typical case of deficit financing. The deficits occur mainly in war and recession. For ex-ample, during World War II, net investment was extremely small. The allocation of resources was largely determined by direct controls; private saving was very large, yet private investment had to be kept small because the materials could not be spared for building private plants and equipment. Thus, the debt financing of World War II probably did not cut investment. In the case of recession and depression, one would expect the general stimulating effects of the deficit to raise rather than to cut investment.

Investment may also be reduced by the presence of an existing public debt. Consumers may consider their bond holdings to be part of their wealth without

---

[1] But think of the tax distortions that would have been caused in the War years if the entire cost of World War II had been met by taxes. Half of all incomes would have had to be taken in taxes. The economy would hardly have been able to function—then how would the war have been won?

considering their offsetting debt obligations as taxpayers. This would make them feel wealthier, raise their consumption, and cut their saving. Further, the higher taxes must have some negative influence on investment, although this factor has to be weighed against the high savings propensities of the interest recipients. Finally, the existence of the large debt may have psychological influences on business behavior. If people really get alarmed over the national debt, the loss of confidence might curtail their investment. The significance of this psychological factor is difficult to evaluate.

More Inflation?

The man in the street fears the debt mainly as a source of inflation. The debt represents past outlays that were not matched by taxes, hence it measures past government claims to resources that it could not pay for.

If government engages in debt financing when the economy is already at full employment, it creates an excessive level of demand and causes inflation. Fortunately, this situation has rarely occurred in the U.S. in peacetime. More commonly, our deficits occur when the economy is weak. Even then, there will be some extra price increases if the economy is lifted by extra government demand. But the stimulus to employment and real production should be the major result, with the extra price increase a minor but unhappy by-product.

Does the Debt Shift the Burden of Past Expenditures into the Future?

Apart from output effects that clearly make future generations worse off, is it possible to shift the burden of past expenditures into the future? For a long time, economists thought that it was impossible. An internal debt does not shift the availability and use of resources through time and hence can do no more than reshuffle incomes within future generations. But about 1958, several economists began to develop doubts whether this was the complete analysis.[2] They asked themselves this question. Under bond financing of a war, which individuals of the wartime generation actually bear the burden? (Under tax financing the issue is clear; the wartime taxpayers have to reduce their consumption and thereby release resources for war.) The bond buyers reduce their consumption, but in exchange they obtain a bond that entitles them to increase their consumption at a later date. Thus, they lend to the society the resources to fight the war; but in exchange they obtain a claim to receive interest that permits them to raise their consumption later on. They really have not borne the burden.

Thus, if the individuals of the society can be neatly divided into the wartime bond buyers and postwar taxpayers—a rather arbitrary grouping—and if

---

[2] J. M. Buchanan, *Public Principles of Public Debt* (Homewood, Ill.: Richard D. Irwin, 1958), and W. G. Bowen, R. G. Davis, and D. H. Kopf, "The Public Debt," *American Economic Review*, Vol. 50, September 1960, pp. 701–5.

they then can be identified as "generations," it is in fact possible to shift some of the burden of the war to a future generation, by giving the wartime generation a claim against the income of future taxpayers. (Only some of the burden can be so shifted because the full cost of the war consists of far more than the expenditure of money. The lost lives, the hardships suffered by the troops, the separation of families, the shortages of civilian goods—all these occur regardless of the method of financing.)

It is not clear that the resultant income redistribution is significant as a matter of social policy. Bond ownership and tax payments are not distributed so very differently, so that even in this individual sense there is a certain amount of "I owe it to myself." Nor can the groups be so clearly identified by age and hence by generations. It is certainly not true that the older generation owns all the bonds and the younger generation pays the taxes. Furthermore, the bonds may be passed on as inheritance, just as the tax liabilities continue.

Does this resultant income redistribution really constitute a shifting of the burden of earlier expenditures to the future? If you think only of the real resources, it does not because the war has still been fought by the older generation and the resources withdrawn from the private economy during that time. Nor is there any change in the output available in the future, leaving aside the minor output and investment effects. But in an individual sense, there is some shifting of the burden because future generations are required to pay interest to the people who acquired the bonds during the war and to their inheritors. Had the older generation been forced to pay taxes instead, this compulsory redistribution would not occur at the later date. So, the method of financing a war does influence who finally pays for it.

SUMMARY

America's national debt is now over $450 billion, or $2,180 for every man, woman, and child in the country. Most of this debt was incurred during war, most of the remainder was due to budget deficits in periods of unemployment. Although the debt is very large, it has been shrinking in relation to GNP partly because of real growth of output, partly because the rise in the price level has reduced the real value of the debt. The federal debt has also become a smaller part of the total debt in the economy, as private and state and local borrowing have risen rapidly through most of the postwar period.

The burden of a public debt is not analogous to that of a private debt. If the debt is internal to the country, interest payments and future retirement of the debt do not require that resources be transferred outside the country. Thus, except for some side effects, the total goods and services available to the economy remain unchanged.

One clear burden of a public debt is any reduction in output that its ex-

95

istence causes. To the extent that the taxes necessary to meet the interest payments have disincentive effects and cause a misallocation of resources, the debt does reduce output. If the debt also reduces investment, the future inherits a smaller capital stock and hence less potential output. A growth of debt can also add to inflation.

Can one generation shift the burden of the costs of its expenditures to a future generation by borrowing? Can the burden of a war be transferred to the future? In one sense, yes; in another, no. The real resources have to be expended at the time the war is fought. However, the wartime generation that chose to borrow rather than to tax itself can collect interest on its bonds from future taxpayers. It can also cash in its bonds and consume the proceeds. Thus, debt financing rather than tax financing gives the wartime generation a future claim against the income of taxpayers.

Managing Aggregate Demand:

Fiscal Policy

for Economic Stability

CHAPTER EIGHT

So far, this book has been chiefly concerned with the long-term objectives of equity, efficiency, and growth. But much of public finance is concerned with short-run matters—the influence of government on total purchasing power, the use of the budget to fight recession and inflation. Changes in taxes and expenditures that aim at the short-run goals of full employment and price-level stability are usually called *fiscal policy*. This chapter examines the theory of fiscal policy, which derives from the general framework of national income analysis.[1] The relation to monetary policy is shown, and the limits of policies that seek to manage aggregate demand are discussed.

THE THEORY OF FISCAL POLICY

To see the role of government budgets in relation to the determination of the short-run output of the economy, let us first recall the determination of national income in the hypothetical situation in which there is no government budget. Figure 8–1 summarizes the national income determination process. Line C is the consumption-GNP relation, which shows the consumption expenditures that will be made out of different levels of Gross National Income. There will also be some specific level of investment, and if we add it to consumption ($C + I$), we get the total level of spending, or "aggregate demand," generated out of each level of income. The equilibrium level of GNP, where total spend-

97

---

[1] See Charles L. Schultze, *National Income Analysis*, this Series, especially Chapters 2 and 3.

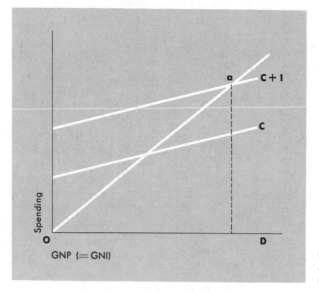

FIG. 8–1 Determination of equilibrium GNP: no government.

ing by households and businesses equals total income and production, is at the point *a* in Fig. 8–1. If the full employment level of GNP is *OD*, equilibrium is below full employment in this example.

Suppose we now bring the government budget into the analysis. Expenditures add to public spending; taxes reduce private spending. Personal taxes reduce disposable income directly, other taxes may be shifted to the consumer via higher prices and reduce the real value of income. Consequently, the consumption-GNP relation is shifted downward. Furthermore, taxes also reduce investment. Thus, the total spending line is shifted downward by the reduction in consumption and investment. It is shifted upward by the government spending.

The budget can raise or lower the equilibrium level of GNP compared to the hypothetical no-government situation. Figure 8–2 shows the new equilibrium. C' is the consumption-GNP relation after taxes have cut disposable income; $C' + I'$ adds the new, lower level of investment; $C' + I' + G$ adds government expenditure to derive the new total spending line. Equilibrium GNP is at *b*. This turns out to be greater than the level *OE* of our no-government case, showing the budget to be a positive influence on effective demand. But this result depends on the magnitude of expenditures and taxes, and on their characteristics.

The fiscal policy implications of national income analysis can be expressed as a series of propositions:

An increase in government expenditures raises GNP. The size of this increase is determined by the multiplier. The additional dollar of government expenditures purchases a dollar of goods and services and becomes the income of households (wages, interest, and rent), of businessmen (profits), and of government (additional tax revenue). Some of these incomes will be respent, the

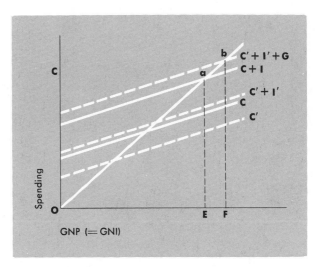

FIG. 8–2 Equilibrium level of GNP compared to a hypothetical no-government situation.

exact amount depending on the marginal spending propensities of the income recipients. Assuming, just for the moment, that neither business nor government spend any of their extra income, and assuming that households spend 90 cents out of every additional dollar of income, we get the following sequence. Let business and government receive 40 cents out of a dollar of extra expenditure. Consumers will spend nine-tenths of the remaining 60 cents, or 54 cents. Assume that these 54 cents of consumption spending will again be divided in the same pattern, yielding households an additional 32 cents of income; they will spend 29 cents for consumption in the next round, and so on. The total effect will be $1 + 54¢ + 29¢ + 16¢ + . . . , a total of $2.18. Thus, for every additional dollar of government expenditures, total GNP is increased by $2.18. And remember that no allowance was made for additional investment out of the increased profits, or for more government spending out of the extra tax revenues. Figure 8–3 shows this multiplier process, with the numerals indicating the succeeding rounds as the new equilibrium level of GNP is approached.

An increase in taxes reduces GNP. The size of the decrease depends on the multiplier. Suppose that taxes are increased by a dollar falling proportionately on household and business income. Households will pay 60 cents, businesses 40 cents. Consumer spending will fall 54 cents in the first round, 29 cents in the second, and so on, as in the preceding example. The resultant sequence, 54¢ + 29¢ + 16¢ + . . . , adds up to a total multiplier on a tax change of $1.18.

Notice that this tax multiplier is just 1 less than the expenditure multiplier (and of opposite sign, of course). This result has a simple explanation. The repercussion effects after the first round are the same; but the government purchase of goods and services was a direct component of effective demand and of GNP, whereas the initial round of the tax payment was simply a transfer of purchasing power that does not count as GNP. The difference of precisely 1 between the

99

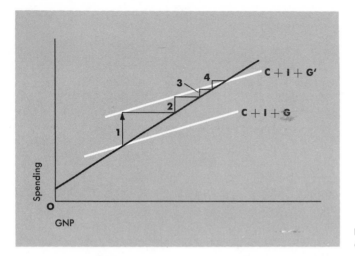

FIG. 8–3 The multiplier process.

expenditure and tax multipliers depends on the assumption that the same marginal propensity to consume applies to the taxpayers as to the income recipients of the government expenditures; and as we shall see below, this is an assumption that is not likely to hold precisely. Nevertheless, it is an important truth that $1 of taxation does not neutralize $1 of expenditures. Unlike the government expenditures, part of the taxes would have been saved rather than spent, and a multiplier has to be applied to this difference. Thus, we add a third principle: *A balanced increase in the level of a budget, with both expenditures and taxes rising by the same amount, changes the level of GNP, normally raising it.*

DEFICITS AND SURPLUSES:
AUTOMATIC AND DISCRETIONARY CHANGES

The actual record of the federal budget (on National Income and Product Account) is shown in Fig. 8–4, along with the unemployment rate. You can see that huge deficits were incurred in recession, a mixture of smaller surpluses and deficits at the other times. Because deficits represent additions to total spending (the government adds more through spending than it subtracts through taxation), the movements in the budget have, broadly speaking, added to economic stability. But in interpreting the raw deficit and surplus figures, this distinction has to be kept in mind:

Some of the changes in the budget are automatic; others are discretionary. As GNP falls, personal incomes and the sales profits of business decline, automatically cutting government revenues. The government is everyone's partner through its taxes, and when private incomes shrink, government income shrinks

100

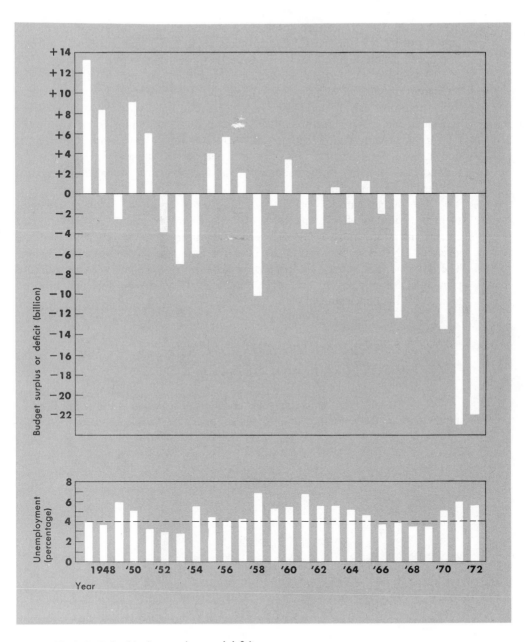

FIG. 8–4 Federal budget surpluses and deficits.

as well. Some categories of expenditures, particularly unemployment and welfare benefits, automatically increase in response to a decline in GNP. Because of falling taxes and rising expenditures, a decline in GNP pushes the budget toward

101

deficit, a rise in GNP toward surplus. As a rule of thumb, for every billion dollars of extra GNP, the federal budget gains about $300 million of extra surplus or reduced deficit. Figure 8–5, line *AA*, shows this relationship.

The taxes and expenditures that exhibit this response have been called *automatic stabilizers*. Although they place the government in deficit, they serve as a cushion for private purchasing power. Back in the 1920s, when government was small and before unemployment insurance, a substantial corporate profits tax, and a broadly levied income tax, there was much less automatic stabilization in the federal budget. This change is perhaps the most significant cause of the increased stability of the economy today and the strongest insurance against another major depression.

The budget can also be changed by *discretionary policies* of government, such as action to change tax rates or expenditure programs. A discretionary change alters the relationship between budget surpluses and deficits and the levels of GNP. Fig. 8–5 shows the effect of a restrictive discretionary change. The new line, *BB*, reflects an increase in tax rates or a reduction in expenditure programs; for any given level of economic activity, the surplus will now be greater (or the deficit smaller).

THE FULL EMPLOYMENT BUDGET,
FISCAL DRAG, AND FISCAL DIVIDENDS

Because the budget surplus or deficit of a period is the result both of movements in the economy and of discretionary policies, one cannot identify

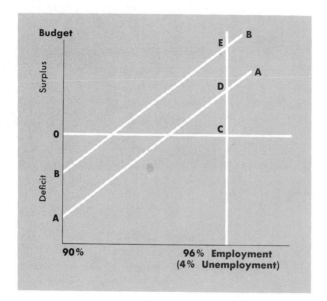

FIG. 8–5 Effect of discretionary change on the budget.

actual budget policy from the historical record of surpluses and deficits. A deficit in recession may not be the result of policy as much as of the shrinking tax base. A surplus during a boom may be produced by the economy rather than deliberate policy choices. To disentangle these elements, the concept of the full employment surplus (or deficit) has been invented. It refers to the surplus or deficit in the budget that would occur if the economy were at full employment. The difference between the full employment surplus and the actual surplus or deficit is then attributable to the automatic budget response to the deviations of the economy from the full employment level. In Fig. 8–5, the vertical distance *CD* measures this full employment surplus under policy *AA*. By looking at full employment surpluses of different budget structures, one can compare just how restrictive or expansionary these budgets are. Thus, the more restrictive budget policy *BB* produces a full employment surplus that is greater than *CD*. The discretionary policy change added *DE* to the full employment surplus. (*Full employment* is usually defined as the condition where unemployment is no greater than the frictional level.)

Figure 8–6 shows the full employment surpluses of the last 18 years. You can see that if there had been continuous full employment, the federal budget would have been in surplus from 1954 to 1965. The full employment surplus moved counter-cyclically, but very much less so than the actual budget surpluses and deficits.

The full employment surplus has a tendency to grow. At full employment, the potential of the American economy grows by about 4 percent. In response, total tax revenues rise by about $18 billion a year. If expenditures were kept absolutely constant, normal economic growth would therefore raise the full employment surplus by $18 billion a year. Such an increase would retard the growth of private purchasing power. Walter Heller has dubbed this phenomenon *fiscal drag*.

The emergence of fiscal drag can be seen in Fig. 8–6. In the second half of the 1950s, expenditures rose a lot less than normal revenue growth, and tax rates were not lowered. As a result of the fiscal drag from these rising full employment surpluses, the economy suffered excess unemployment for eight years. In 1964, personal and corporate income tax rates were cut; the full employment surplus became small, and the economy began a rapid advance that carried it to full employment in the next two years. By 1966, the economy was advancing so rapidly that discretionary policy began to lean the other way to raise the full employment surplus.

To avoid fiscal drag, the normal revenue growth of $18 billion a year must be allocated to higher expenditures, or to lower tax rates. There will be times when the economy is too buoyant and some fiscal drag will be desirable. But in the long run, normal revenue growth must be used, or else the economy is slowed down.

Heller has called this revenue growth, which is the product of an expanding economy, the *fiscal dividend*. It represents an opportunity to choose among desirable alternatives: to improve the quality and quantity of public services, to

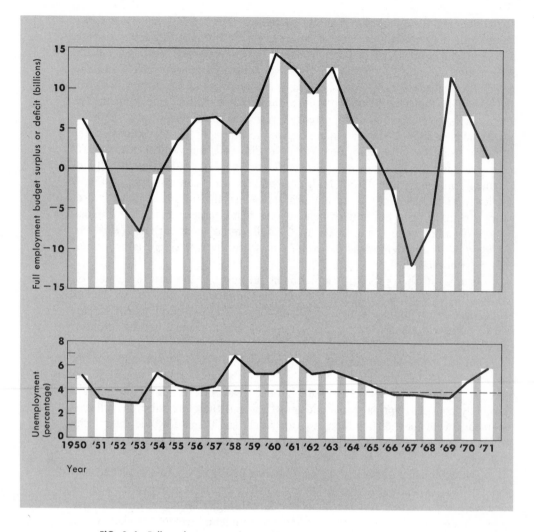

FIG. 8–6 Full employment surpluses, 1954–1971.

step up grants to state and local governments or transfer payments to the poor, or to reduce tax rates.

In more recent years, the budget has become overcommitted and there may be a tendency for the political process to let the full employment budget drift into deficit. Since 1966, surpluses have been short-lived, as new expenditure programs and repeated tax reductions have more than spent the fiscal dividend.

The full employment budget can be used as a simple tool of analysis, bringing planned discretionary policy changes and the normal fiscal dividend together. Table 8–1 shows a hypothetical example of such budget planning. It

Table 8–1   A TYPICAL FULL EMPLOYMENT BUDGET (billions of dollars)

	Effect on Full Employment Surplus
Revenues	
Fiscal dividend (normal revenue growth)	+18
Scheduled increase in social security payroll taxes	+ 6
Expiration of excise taxes	− 2
Expenditures	
Normal increase of social security outlays	− 5
Increases in formula-grant programs and other automatic expenditure increases	− 4
Discretionary changes in spending programs	− 7
Change in Full Employment Surplus	+ 6

lists various automatic and discretionary expenditure and tax changes. Many of these changes are not made to promote a correct overall fiscal policy. The changes may be due to population growth, larger outlays in the matching grant-in-aid programs, changing military needs, or past legislative actions scheduling present tax or expenditure changes. Indeed, much of each year's budget is predetermined in various ways. But the full employment budget brings all these discretionary and automatic changes together and adds them up to identify the net change in the full employment surplus. In our example, a fiscal drag of $6 billion emerges. Whether it is appropriate, or whether it should be used for some further fiscal dividend, will depend upon the outlook for the economy as a whole, whether or not the broad objectives of full employment and price stability require a mild fiscal drag at the particular time.

SOME COMPLICATIONS

The prescriptions of fiscal theory are straightforward enough—cut taxes, raise expenditures to expand the economy; raise taxes, cut expenditures to contract it. The multiplier reveals how large the changes must be to reach full employment at stable prices. Then why is there so much controversy about fiscal policies? And why we don't follow the rules and avoid unemployment and inflation? Before we leave this subject, we had best examine some of the qualifications to the theory, some practical difficulties of implementing it, and some of the other ideas and budget principles that are being advanced in the continuing national debate over our national budget.

Not all expenditures have the same multiplier effects. Transfer payments do not constitute a direct demand for goods and services. Just as a part of taxes reduces saving rather than spending, so part of the transfer expenditures goes into saving. With the initial round of assured direct purchase of goods and services absent, a lower multiplier is likely.[2]

---

[2] If the transfer recipients have the same marginal propensity to consume as taxpayers, a balanced increase of taxes and transfer payments would have no effect on total demand whatsoever.

Nor will the households through whom the various rounds of the multiplier pass all have the same marginal propensity to consume. We know that upper-income families save more so that the multiplier may be larger or smaller depending on who receives the income. During the Great Depression, it was believed that the economy could be stimulated significantly simply by redistributing income—taxing the upper-income, high-saving groups, paying benefits to low-income, low-saving groups. The resultant effect on spending was called the *redistribution multiplier.* Empirical studies, on the whole, have cast doubt on the possibilities of this procedure. Marginal propensities to consume are high right up through all the income brackets that have millions of people in them, and the amount of income that could be redistributed from the high-saving group is small.

Some government expenditures will displace private expenditures, rather than add to them. For example, a government-built hydroelectric power dam inevitably displaces some private investment that would have been made to meet the power needs of the area. When the government purchases home mortgages in large quantities to stimulate house building, many of these mortgages would have been financed privately and the homes would have been built anyway.

Government spending may also jolt business confidence. In the 1930s, there was fear that the sheer growth of government and the possibility of nationalization would discourage business investment. But by now, we have all grown accustomed to big government. And the knowledge that the government does have responsibility for moderating the business cycle shores up business confidence.

Not all tax changes have the same multiplier effects. There may be differences in the marginal propensities to consume among taxpayers. As long as the tax change is not concentrated in the very top brackets, this is not likely to amount to much as a quantitative matter. But a tax on the rich will hit savings harder, consumption less.

A temporary tax cut may not be as effective as a permanent reduction. Some economists believe that consumption out of temporary or "windfall" income is less than out of income expected to be received regularly.[3] If this is correct, then a lower multiplier has to be applied to a temporary tax cut.

Tax changes other than changes in personal income taxes do not fit the fiscal theory of the multiplier so neatly, and other analyses must be added. For example, an increase in sales tax rates involves other issues. First, to whom is the burden of the tax shifted? If the tax is borne by consumers, it reduces their real purchasing power just like an income tax. If part of the burden is shifted to the workers producing the taxed product through lower wage payments, this is also like an income tax. Some of the tax may fall on the profits of the industry, leading to a reduction in investment. Further, because a sales tax is levied on

[3] This position is advanced in M. Friedman, *The Theory of the Consumption Function,* National Bureau of Economic Research, 1957.

consumption only, it may lead consumers to substitute saving for consumption, thus producing an additional cut in spending.

Suppose the corporation income tax is changed. First, the shifting and incidence problem has to be resolved. Who really pays—the business, the consumer, or the worker? In so far as the incidence falls on business profits, the initial effect on spending will not depend on the multiplier that measures consumption effects, but on the influence of corporate profits on investment (see Chapter Six). Does an extra dollar of corporation income tax reduce investment by 10 cents or by a dollar? So far, there is no agreement on this question. We do know that the effect will be greater when business is short of investible funds in relation to investment opportunities than when corporations have a lot of liquid assets. Thus, the effect of this kind of tax change on total spending depends on the circumstances during a particular period.

The financing of deficits can have a restrictive effect. Suppose that government is fighting a recession by raising expenditures and cutting taxes, thereby creating a sizable deficit. This deficit has to be financed somehow because government, like anyone else, has to pay its bills. To do so, it sells securities, going to the capital market like any other borrower. It thereby competes with private investment by making it more difficult for private borrowers to obtain investible funds. In a period of tight credit, private borrowing may be substantially decreased by government borrowing. The negative multipliers on the reduction of private investment may offset a significant part of the positive multipliers arising from the government's tax and spending policy.

Usually, this offset will be small. The Federal Reserve System will have the same policy goals as the rest of the government, and when the budget is put into deficit to stimulate the economy, the Reserve System will be pursuing an easy money policy. It will keep bank reserves ample through open-market operations or reduced reserve requirements, thus making it possible for both private and public borrowers to obtain funds readily and at moderate interest cost. Nevertheless, if the Federal Reserve works at cross purposes with the fiscal policy, it can offset the stimulating effect of reduced taxes or higher expenditures.

Practical difficulties: time lags. The delays in diagnosing recessions and inflations and of then devising and executing fiscal policy measures are perhaps the biggest obstacle to the effective use of discretionary fiscal policies. First, there is the *recognition lag*, the several months that pass before analysts agree that a recession or an inflation in fact exists. The *decision lag* follows, the months during which the president and his advisers make up their minds just what to do, the period of consideration by the Congress, plus the additional months in which the expenditure programs or the tax changes actually become effective. Finally, there is the *expenditure lag*, the period before the full economic impact of the successive multiplier rounds takes place.

Practical difficulties: forecasting errors. Diagnosis may not only be tardy but also wrong. The ups and downs of the post-war business cycle have been so slight and sudden that it has been difficult to predict them accurately. Short-run

107

forecasters closely follow hundreds of statistical indicators that show the direction of movement of the economy, and construct elaborate econometric models to discover the coming business-cycle patterns. Nevertheless, forecasting remains an uncertain art. Discretionary fiscal policies, if they are to contribute to economic stability through quick action, must be based on correct forecasts. If analysts could foresee a coming recession or inflation, preventive policies could be pursued.

In fact, few have succeeded in predicting turning points in the business cycle. The best that we have been able to do so far is to diagnose them promptly after they have happened. This forecasting difficulty has led some observers to conclude that fiscal policy should rely exclusively on automatic stabilizers, which swing into action without explicit diagnosis through the working of the economy itself. However, discretionary policies undertaken after the recession (or inflation) has been diagnosed may still contribute to economic stability.

OTHER BUDGET PRINCIPLES:
THE ANNUALLY BALANCED BUDGET

Modern fiscal theory requires that at some times the budget be in surplus, at others in deficit. Only by accident would precise balance be the exactly correct budget policy. Yet, the idea of balancing expenditures with revenues for every year continues to have immense appeal and crops up without end in speeches and on editorial pages. Even political leaders who understand and accept modern fiscal theory find themselves very much on the defensive when the budget is in deficit.

Why do the older ideas die so slowly? Do they possibly contain some germ of validity? One thing is certain. If the federal government pursued a rigid budget-balancing policy, insisting on precise balance each year regardless of the movements in the private economy, it would lead to disaster. It would mean that tax rates would be increased and expenditures slashed in recession, and taxes cut and spending increased in inflation. In the early days of the Great Depression, both Presidents Hoover and Roosevelt deliberately sought to restore budget balance, even as unemployment grew very large. They raised taxes in 1932, 1934, and 1935, and enforced strict economy in the ordinary budget. A humane response to the desperate needs of the unemployed, first by Hoover and then more extensively by Roosevelt, led them to establish various relief and public-works programs, helping to swell the depression-induced deficits. But the total discretionary fiscal policy of the 1930s, as measured by the full employment deficits and surpluses, reflected the fear of unbalanced budgets and kept the government from an all-out antidepression fiscal policy. This was a contributing factor to the depth and persistence of the depression.

108

Then why do the ideas persist? First, because we draw simple analogies between our personal finances and the government's finances. We know that when our expenditures exceed our income, we pile up debts; a day of reckoning comes when we have to cut down our standard of living to pay the creditors. The preceding chapter discussed the rather different and more limited burden of a public debt. Compared to the fruits of a proper fiscal policy, the changes in the debt are a small cost.

It is also widely believed that the deficits cause inflation, and that to abandon the balanced budget is to let governments pursue never-ceasing inflationary policies. Now, it is true that deficits add to total demand, and in some circumstances this will be inflationary. But increased demand should not lead to price increases so long as there is unemployed labor and idle capital; thus, deficits should not be inflationary in periods of underemployment. If the economy has an inflationary bias caused by concentrations of market power in the hands of companies and unions, then deficits that restore full employment will also produce inflation. But here the trouble lies not in the deficit but in the monopoly elements in the structure of the economy's markets.

Another reason for the continued support of the annually balanced budget is the belief that it is the only principle that limits the growth of government expenditures. Adam Smith favored budget balancing on these grounds. Royal borrowing paid for wasteful court life, depriving the business classes of much-needed credit to finance the trade and investment that was the basis of economic growth. Today, it is not kings but politicians who are supposed to be "reckless spenders." Budget balancing every year forces politicians to face up to the tax cost of expenditures, and because increases in tax rates are unpopular, it helps confine the expenditure rise to normal revenue growth.

Although budget-balancing may reduce total spending, it does not assure efficiency or an end to waste. If there is waste in government, in such fields as agriculture, stockpiling, foreign aid, or even defense, a balanced budget will not eliminate it. Wasteful expenditures, on the whole, have not resulted from general fiscal looseness but from powerful pressure groups (both the private beneficiaries and the public bureaucracies that administer the programs) and from the lack of pressure for efficiency in the absence of competition and the profit motive. Wider application of economic analysis to public expenditures, as sketched in Chapter Two, is a more constructive approach to efficiency in government and permits a modern fiscal policy to function.

BALANCING THE FULL EMPLOYMENT BUDGET: THE CED PLAN BECOMES OFFICIAL POLICY

Recognizing that sound budget policy requires both counter-cyclical variation in surpluses and deficits as well as some principles to assure fiscal discipline, the Committee for Economic Development, an organization of business leaders, proposed in 1947 that a new budget principle be adopted. They recommended that the level of expenditures be determined on the basis of long-term merits and that tax rates be set so that balance, or even a small surplus would be produced if full employment prevailed. It was expected that this budget principle would produce a balanced budget over the full course of business cycles, with the surpluses of strong booms offsetting the deficits in recession.

This policy recommendation was noteworthy on several grounds. First, it indicated that a modern, counter-cyclical fiscal policy was acceptable to an important segment of the business community. Second, the policy rejects discretionary policies and relies completely on the automatic flexibility of the budget. The CED felt that the time lags in discretionary fiscal measures were too great and forecasting errors too serious. They also felt that a discretionary fiscal policy made the environment for business decisions more uncertain, as businessmen, besides running their ordinary risks, would have to guess about government policy. Finally, the principle preserves the requirement on politicians to balance new expenditure programs with new revenues, because the rule of a small surplus at full employment requires the matching of expenditures with revenues. In this way, it was hoped that a modern counterpart of the principle of the annually balanced budget could be established.

In 1971, the Nixon Administration adopted the principle of balance in the full employment budget as the official target of fiscal policy. The government's reasoning was very much along the CED's lines. Initially, the new principle meant that the government was content to run a very large actual deficit in recession. But in subsequent years, the major impact of the policy will be to require tax increases to pay for rapidly rising expenditures.

The principle can be criticized. Automatic stabilization may not be enough. Depending on conditions in the private economy, the CED policy might leave the economy with substantial unemployment or inflation. When the private economy is particularly buoyant, with investment demand high, and, say, automobile sales booming, correct stabilization policy may require a large surplus in the full employment budget. When private demand is weak, stabilization may require a deficit in the full employment budget. There is no assurance that a budget that would balance at hypothetical full employment will actually produce full employment. As for fiscal discipline, it is questionable whether wasteful expenditures are kept in check even by the annually balanced budget; a hypothetical budget balance never confirmed by dollar-and-cents accounting would have an even slighter effect. Nevertheless, the policy would have worked tolerably well in the last 20 years, probably better than actual policy a good part of the time. And that is not a small recommendation.

ACTUAL FISCAL POLICY
AGAINST RECESSION

Judged by movements in the full employment surplus of the Federal budget, fiscal policy has been stabilizing, although the changes have fallen far short of the performance that modern fiscal principles would prescribe. Figure 8–7 shows the full employment surpluses during the most recent four recessions.

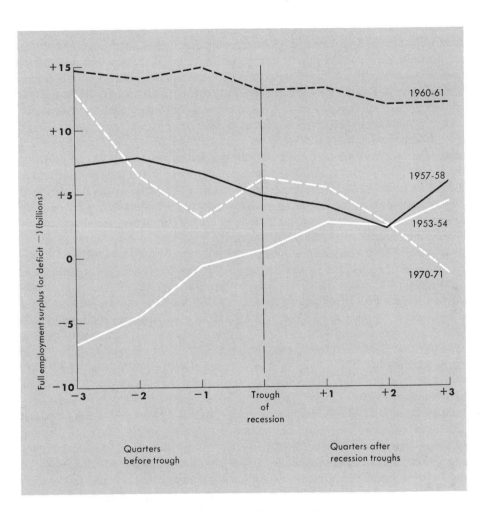

FIG. 8–7 Full employment budget surpluses in four recessions.

In three out of four cases, an excessive full-employment surplus contributed to the coming of recession. Fiscal policy did move toward stimulus once the recession was diagnosed.

On the whole, the use of discretionary tax policy against recession has been disappointing. In the 1949 and 1954 recessions, the Congress did enact tax reductions, but for reasons unrelated to the recession. The Congress eliminated temporary taxes imposed during war and did so over the objections of the Administration.

The most critical failure of tax policy was in the recession of 1958, which was the most severe of the postwar setbacks and the only one in which real fears of a depression began to spread among businessmen and consumers. A tax cut was debated at length during the trough of the recession. But when the economy gave clear signals that some kind of recovery had begun, the government decided firmly against a tax cut. It was generally believed, despite the teaching of modern macroeconomics, that once the economy entered the recovery phase, it was likely to return to full employment. In actuality, the economy did not overcome the heavy fiscal drag of a large and rising full employment surplus, and unemployment remained about 5 percent in succeeding years.

In the recession of 1960–61, discretionary tax policy once again was not used. The process leading to inaction followed the previous pattern. By the time the Kennedy administration took office and it was officially acknowledged that there was a recession, there were ample signs that recovery was on the way. Despite the reemergence of a premature full-employment surplus, the government was hesitant to propose tax reduction so long as there was a reasonable chance that full employment might be reached through private recovery alone. In the most recent recession, 1969–71, the tax action was taken and was a major factor in the mildness of the recession. The tax surcharges levied to finance the Vietnam war were due to expire, the Tax Reform Act of 1969 was scheduled to reduce tax rates, and so the government had the opportunity to use a stimulating tax policy by accelerating reductions that had already been scheduled. These changes included reductions in personal and corporate income taxes, restoration of the investment tax credit, as well as the termination of the excise tax on automobiles.

On the expenditure side, the actual record of discretionary policy also shows only limited successes. It has been found, over and over again, that the delays in reaching political decisions on new expenditure programs are so long that the recession has come and gone before the programs become effective. Existing programs can be accelerated, but the actual history shows that the magnitudes of such expenditure changes are very small. For example, a detailed study of the 1958 recession, when there was particularly heavy reliance on the acceleration of expenditure programs, showed that the automatic part of fiscal policy was several times more important than the discretionary changes. And what discretionary changes there were came rather late.[4]

The greatest promise on the expenditure side is in the field of transfer payments. The unemployment insurance system has been improved considerably, with benefits higher and the duration of eligibility extended in recession. Liberalization of the welfare programs and improvements in the social security system can also be timed to aid economic recovery.

In summary, the automatic stabilizers play a critical role in protecting the economy against the risk of having recession turn into depression. Government revenues fall quickly and some categories of expenditures rise automatically, to

---

[4] See Wilfred Lewis, Jr., *Federal Fiscal Policy in the Post-War Recessions* (Washington, D.C.: The Brookings Institution, 1962).

a degree that acts as a major buffer between levels of overall activity and private incomes. The growth of the automatic stabilizers is probably the most important change improving the macro performance of the American economy.

On the other hand, the record of discretionary tax and expenditure policy is disappointing. Actions were usually taken rather late, with a considerable lag between the beginnings of recession and its recognition.

ACTUAL FISCAL POLICY
DURING INFLATION

The United States has experienced four inflations since World War II: the post-World War II inflation, the inflation during the Korean War; the creeping inflation of the mid-fifties, and the inflation associated with the Vietnam War that began in 1965. Our review of fiscal policy in practice would not be complete without a quick look at its role in these episodes.

The inflation of 1945–1948 accompanied the astonishingly smooth and successful reconversion of the economy from military to civilian production at the end of World War II. As the federal government cut the share of GNP that it absorbed, from 42 percent in 1944 to less than 7 percent in 1947, it reduced wartime taxes substantially, but much less than expenditures. A deficit of $55 billion in 1944 was converted to a surplus of $12 billion in 1947. This enormous swing could not eliminate inflation because private demand was extremely strong. Families reunited after the war had pressing needs for housing, cars, and appliances, and they possessed the wartime savings to convert these backlogs into effective demand. Considerable inflation was suppressed in wartime through price, wage, and rent controls; and when these controls were removed, wages and prices moved to new equilibrium levels. No fiscal policy could have averted this inflation, but fiscal policy made a substantial contribution in limiting the inflation and bringing it to an end.

The Korean War inflation was largely psychological. Consumers, businesses, and governments all over the world promptly hoarded commodities, driving world material prices up sharply and causing wholesale and retail prices to rise by over 10 percent in a year. Price and wage controls were imposed, but only after much of the price increase had already occurred. Fiscal policy was the main instrument of antiinflationary policy during the crucial early stages of the war. In September, 1950, both personal and corporate income tax rates were increased, and an excess profits tax was imposed. A year later, as military expenditures increased, income taxes were raised once more, and excise taxes on luxuries boosted. Thus, discretionary action was prompt and vigorous. It could

113

not stop the inflation in its tracks because of the intensity of the psychological pressure, but it reduced the amount of inflation and permitted the diversion of resources to war purposes.

The inflation of the mid-fifties was in some respects the most frustrating for policy. Excess demand did not permeate the entire economy but was confined to a few sectors—the durable-goods industries, such as autos and machinery, and some services, such as medical care. Concentrations of market powers also played a role, particularly in the later stages of the cycle when expansion was slow, yet prices and wages continued to rise. All in all, it was a period in which a state just a shade below full employment was combined with considerable inflation, our first major experience with the unemployment-inflation dilemma.

Monetary policy carried much of the burden of fighting inflation in the mid-fifties. The Federal Reserve tightened credit, though only after a considerable time lag. No discretionary tax changes were made, expenditures rose slowly, and the budget moved into substantial surplus. Thus, although virtually no explicit discretionary fiscal measures were undertaken, the automatic stabilizers, particularly rising tax revenues, gradually gave the budget an antiinflationary impact. The peculiar nature of the inflation, its concentration in a few sectors, and its cost-push element made this inflation particularly intractable to general fiscal (or monetary) policies.

The most recent inflation, the worst such experience in our modern history, developed after six years of price and cost stability. With the utilization rates of industry rising from 85 to 91 percent, some industrial material prices began to rise in 1965. Food prices rose quickly, and gradually industrial goods prices also moved up. Wages, which had risen little more than productivity until 1966, rose more rapidly in response to low unemployment, rising food prices, and high profits, thereby raising unit labor costs.

The fundamental force behind this inflation was the rapid rise in demand fueled by booming auto sales, a capital goods boom, and military spending for the war in Vietnam. Initially, the burden of restraining demand fell mainly on monetary policy. Government expenditures, both military and civilian, were rising rapidly, and tax action was limited to the acceleration of payment schedules and the rescission of reductions of excise taxes. The automatic stabilizers operated as usual, raising revenues sharply but no more than expenditures, leaving the full employment budget virtually in balance in 1966. In the fall of 1966, discretionary fiscal policy entered a more vigorous phase. The investment credit on equipment was suspended, the accelerated depreciation methods were suspended on buildings, and the growth of civilian spending was checked. In early 1967, broader tax action was requested by the president, and a 10 percent surcharge on personal and corporate income taxes was enacted effective mid–1968. Fiscal action came much too late. With unemployment below 3.5 percent, the full employment budget had been allowed to fall into a sizable deficit.

THE PROPER MIX OF FISCAL
AND MONETARY POLICIES

This brief historical account illustrates that fiscal and monetary policy can be substituted for one another to promote full employment or to check inflation. The proper fiscal policy depends on the current monetary policy; conversely, the monetary authorities must take fiscal policy into account in devising their own actions. Figure 8–8 shows the simultaneous relations of the two forms of policies to full employment. The upper set of diagrams shows the determination of the money supply that will produce full employment. M_{FE} is that quantity of money that results in an interest rate just sufficiently low to bring about

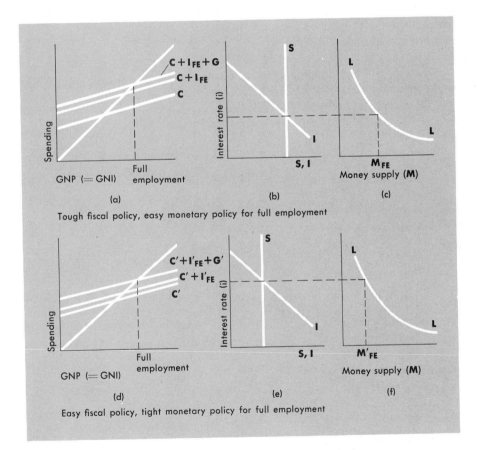

FIG. 8–8 The mix of fiscal and monetary policies.

the volume of investment that absorbs the full employment volume of savings.[5] But the consumption schedule in Fig. 8–8 (a) is based on given tax rates. The government spending G assumes a specific budget.

Now suppose that fiscal policy becomes easier; tax rates are lowered; government spending is increased. Then, aggregate demand increases as C and G become larger (Fig. 8–8 (d)). If the economy is to remain at the full employment point of GNP and not go beyond to excess demand inflation, investment must be reduced. If M is reduced sufficiently, i will rise, cutting investment to its new, lower full employment level. Figure 8–9 portrays these relationships more generally. Each point on the diagram represents a particular combination of fiscal and monetary policy, as measured by its full employment deficit (or surplus) and quantity of money. Some of the points will result in a GNP just equal to its full employment level; all such points are on the line aa. It has the curvature shown because the more a particular policy is used, beyond some point it becomes less effective. Particularly in the case of money, ever larger increases make the economy so liquid that interest rates will cease to fall. At the other extreme, if money is made so scarce that the financial system becomes disorganized, expansionary fiscal policy will work badly.

Because different combinations of policies can promote full employment equally effectively, the best choice can be determined on the basis of other criteria. Of course, in any particular situation, one or another of the policies may be more feasible for administrative or political reasons. But the choice of policy

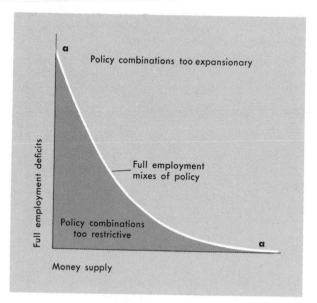

FIG. 8–9 Mixes of full employment policies.

[5] See J. S. Duesenberry, *Money and Credit*, 3rd ed., this Series, for fuller exposition.

mix also makes a difference to the accomplishment of various economic objectives.

First, the impact on economic growth may differ. Excessive reliance on restrictive monetary policy will cut the rate of capital formation because high interest rates reduce investment. Particularly if fiscal policy is easy on the taxation of households, the share of GNP going into investment may be too low.

On the other hand, a tight monetary policy is beneficial for equilibrium in the balance of payments. Capital tends to flow from low- to high-interest countries. There is a large pool of short-term money that moves to whatever world financial centers have the highest interest rates. Even the long-term capital markets have become so internationalized that a low-interest rate policy attracts foreign borrowers who draw American capital abroad. With the U.S. international payments balance in deficit in the last decade, we have had to maintain relatively high interest rates to defend our currency and have relied relatively more on fiscal policy to achieve an expansionary policy mix.

Considerations of resource allocation and economic structure also determine the most desirable policy combination. Tight monetary policy affects investment in housing very drastically. If a restraining policy mix leans too much toward the money side, home building may be curtailed so sharply that housing shortages could develop, or the policy will be considered inequitable because it singles out one industry for exceptional treatment. Small and new businesses and state and local governments are also often cited as leading sufferers from tight money.

Further, there is a limit to the extent to which monetary policy can be used. If money suddenly becomes very tight, the financial system is dealt such a shock that institutions cannot adjust successfully; some of them may be forced into bankruptcy and broad, financial disturbances may result.

When the policy mix should be expansionary, structural considerations also come into play. If fiscal policy remains restrictive and an increase in the money supply is the main tool for expansion, the growth of credit may become excessive. An expansion that is heavily based on credit expansion is more vulnerable to setbacks than one based on income growth: as credit becomes more available, it not only becomes cheaper; marginal loans are likely to be of lower quality, going into speculative ventures, to borrowers with a high risk of default.

PHILLIPS CURVES AND
THE CHOICE OF OBJECTIVES

So far, we have discussed short-term economic policy as if we could single-mindedly pursue one objective: to boost demand until full employment is reached; to curtail demand to avoid inflation when demand threatens to ex-   **117** ceed the full employment level. Some of the time, that is not a bad description of the situation. From 1958 to 1964, the major problem of short-term policy was to raise demand; in some later years, demand was clearly excessive, and it was the task of policy to restrain it. But there is a broad range of economic performance where things are not so simple, where the objectives conflict, where the economy suffers from rising prices without having achieved full employment.[6]

What is policy to do in this unhappy situation—worsen the inflation by boosting demand to achieve full employment, or create excess unemployment to stabilize prices?

The amount of inflation that is associated with a particular amount of unemployment depends on the market structure of the economy, particularly on the price changes in particular industries associated with various cost and demand changes, and on the increases that workers can obtain at any given level of unemployment. These relations can be summarized in an economy's "Phillips Curve" (named after A. W. Phillips, the English economist who invented it).

Figure 8–10 (a) shows a case where full employment is consistent with price stability; Fig. 8–10 (b) shows the case that is more typical for most countries most of the time. In the full employment range, where unemployment is 3 to 4 percent, prices are increasing 2 to 4 percent, or rather more than can be suffered in silence.

Fiscal and monetary policies that manage the level of aggregate demand can aim at any of the points on the economy's Phillips Curve, but they can do no more. The value judgments of the government will determine whether it will attach a heavy weight to full employment and aim at a point such as *a*, or

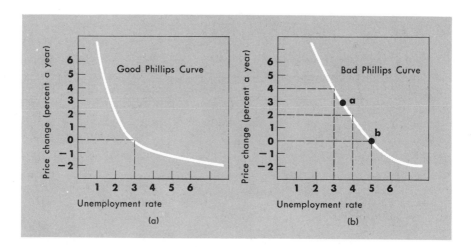

FIG. 8–10 Phillips curves.

[6] See Charles L. Schultze, *National Income Analysis*, 3rd ed. (Englewood Cliffs, N.J.: Prentice-Hall, Inc., 1971), Chapter 5, for further discussion.

whether it chooses to suffer more unemployment for the sake of price stability, as at point *b*.

Short and Long Run Phillips Curves and the Choices for Policy

The Phillips Curve poses the policy option in a stark form, but it omits one particularly critical complexity. In the long run, the tradeoffs are different than in the short run. The rate of wage increase produced by any given unemployment rate depends upon the preceding history of prices. If prices have been stable, workers are not sensitive to inflation, and hence minor changes in consumer prices will have only a small effect on wage claims. On the other hand, once inflation has been underway for some time and workers' families have experienced the impact on their living standards, inflation becomes a central issue of collective bargaining. If the inflation persists long enough, wage claims fully

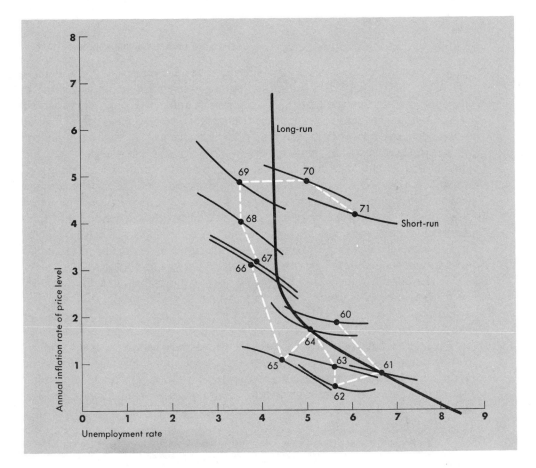

FIG. 8–11   Long- and short-run Phillips curves.

reflect changes in consumer prices and with little or no delay. Businesses, in reaching their pricing decisions, also begin to take the inflation for granted at some point and pass on cost increases, whether of labor, material, or capital, fully and with little delay. Once the economy reaches this point, with wages and prices interacting fully and with little lag, the wage-price spiral takes on an explosive character and the Phillips Curve ceases to have meaning. The curves shift as fast as prices change, becoming steadily worse. Figure 8–11 shows long and short run Phillips Curves as they were estimated in a recent study.

The distinction between short- and long-run Phillips Curves poses a major challenge for economic policy. In principle, governments should consider the long-run impacts of their actions. Should they overstimulate the economy, the social cost is not the movement along the short-term Phillips Curve but the movement along the long-run curve, which is usually worse: an excessively stimulating fiscal policy will produce only mild inflation in the first year or two, but as excess demand persists, the inflation becomes acute. At least, that has been the recent experience of the United States.

Has the Phillips Curve Shifted?

A number of economists have advanced the hypothesis that the Phillips Curve for the United States has shifted for the worse since the mid–1960s.[7] It has long been recognized that the unemployment rates of young, inexperienced workers are higher than for experienced, adult workers. The period from leaving school until the worker finds his initial occupation frequently involves a number of job changes. Also, an inexperienced worker has less knowledge of the job market and greater difficulty in being hired. Since the mid-sixties, young, inexperienced workers have risen greatly in numbers, and hence the average national unemployment rate for any given economic condition has become somewhat greater. To be sure, the typical young worker is better educated today than he was in earlier years, and the percentage of young workers who have not completed high school has fallen sharply. But the problem of finding those initial jobs is compounded by the growth in the numbers of young workers.

The unemployment rates of women are usually higher than the rates for men. A fraction of women want to be part-time workers, and inequality of job opportunity places women at a disadvantage. The participation rate of women in the labor force, that is, the percentage of women of working age who desire to have a job, has risen steadily through the postwar period, as fewer women have remained content to be housewives. As a result, the percentage of the labor force represented by women has risen sharply, and this is another factor raising the national unemployment rate associated with given economic conditions. On the other side, it should be stressed that an increasing number of women are

[7] See G. Perry, "Changing Labor Markets and Inflation," *Brookings Papers on Economic Activity,* 1970:3, and R. J. Gordon, "Inflation in Recession and Recovery," *Brookings Papers on Economic Activity,* 1971:1.

full-time job holders and a rising fraction are heads of households. Thus, the frequent association of women workers as having a looser tie to the labor force becomes increasingly dubious.

Whether the Phillips Curve has shifted for the worse, and if so to what extent, is an issue of more than scientific curiosity. The nation's full-employment targets presumably have to be defined in terms of the attainable range of the Phillips Curve. If the Curve is shifted, it would require a lowering of our unemployment targets—or new kinds of policies.

In the coming years, a challenge to policy will be to achieve a better long-run Phillips Curve. Improvement of the structure of labor and product markets and policies to make private decision makers with market power more responsive to the public interest are important steps in this direction. But fiscal policy itself has an important role to play. Government expenditure policies in such fields as agriculture, stockpiles, housing, labor, and health care inevitably affect prices and costs in the private sector. They should be managed to improve, rather than to worsen, the Phillips Curve. Government programs of human investment in education and training can add to the supply of effective, skilled manpower and reduce the level of frictional unemployment. And tax policies that foster the rapid growth of industrial capacity will make product markets more competitive and thereby reduce upward price pressures.

In the last three decades, economists and politicians have learned to manage fiscal and monetary policies so that the economy can avoid depression or wild inflation. We can remain in the more attractive ranges of the Phillips Curve, where unemployment is limited and price increases mild. But to use the full potential of our economy year after year, our public finance policies must set even higher goals—to improve the economy's structure and to facilitate long-term growth.

SUMMARY

The theory of fiscal policy is a corollary of national income analysis. It views government expenditures as an addition to aggregate demand, taxes a reduction of aggregate demand. Modern fiscal policy requires that government expenditures and taxes be changed to achieve the stabilization objectives of full employment and stable prices. At times, this requires that fiscal policy be expansionary (to raise expenditures and reduce taxes), and at other times to be restrictive (to reduce expenditures and increase taxes). The magnitudes of tax and expenditure changes required to accomplish any particular change in effective demand depend on the multiplier.

A balanced increase in the level of the budget, with both taxes and expenditures rising by the same amount, will normally raise the level of GNP because part of the taxes will have come out of savings while all the expenditures are spent.

In analyzing the historical record of budget deficits and surpluses, automatic changes must be distinguished from discretionary changes. Automatic changes are the result of movements in the private economy. When the economy enters recession, tax bases automatically shrink, yielding less revenue, and some categories of expenditures, such as unemployment benefits, automatically increase. Discretionary changes, on the other hand, are the result of explicit government action, such as changes in the tax rates or the adoption of new spending programs. The concept of the full-employment budget surplus permits the identification of changes in discretionary policy.

The actual management of fiscal policy requires more than a mechanical application of the theory. In each situation, certain complications and qualifications to the theory must be kept in mind.

Not all expenditures have the same multiplier effects. Transfer payments must be distinguished from purchases of goods and services because they do not constitute a direct demand in the initial round of the multiplier process. Not all households have the same marginal propensity to consume, and therefore the multiplier will differ depending on the spending propensities of the recipients. Some expenditures displace private expenditures rather than add to them.

Similarly, not all tax changes have the same multiplier effects. In some instances, the effect on business liquidity and investment is more important than the effect on consumption. Temporary tax changes may also have effects different from permanent tax changes.

The financing of budget deficits can have a restrictive effect, partly offsetting the benefits of an expansionary policy. If monetary policy is not sufficiently erased to permit both private and public borrowers to obtain funds at moderate interest cost, the government borrowing will compete with private borrowing, cutting private investment.

There are also practical difficulties in the use of fiscal policy. Discretionary policy runs into the serious time lags of recognition, decision, and of expenditure effects. Forecasting errors may also reduce its effectiveness.

The annual balanced budget still receives some public support. If rigorously pursued, it would lead to disastrous results for the economy. It does, however, provide some damper on government spending, whereas the strictly counter-cyclical principles of modern fiscal policy do not contain any simple public yardstick that could discipline spending decisions arising out of the political process. The CED proposal of a slightly overbalanced budget at full employment attempts to combine the advantages of modern counter-cyclical policy with fiscal discipline.

Postwar fiscal policy has helped significantly to stabilize the economy. Deficits and surpluses have moved in a counter-cyclical manner, keeping the declines in total private purchasing power about one-half as large as the declines in total GNP.

Much of the larger part of this maintenance of private purchasing power resulted from the workings of the automatic stabilizers. Discretionary policy made a minor contribution to stability. Postwar recessions, however, were brief and mild, and in the event of a more serious decline, discretionary policy could play a larger role.

Fiscal policy against inflation was used most extensively during the Korean War, when it was the main instrument of stabilization policy and tax rates were increased substantially. It did not prevent a largely psychological inflation, but moderated it. During the inflation after World War II, pent-up demands were so great that even a fiscal policy of budget surpluses could do no more than hasten the end of the inflation. The inflation of the mid-fifties was chiefly fought with monetary policy. The most recent inflation was initially fought mainly by monetary policy. Later, fiscal policy was used more fully.

Because both fiscal and monetary policies can influence the level of aggregate demand, any given level of demand can be achieved through a variety of combinations of the two kinds of policies. Whether relatively tight fiscal policy combined with relatively easy monetary policy is preferable to the opposite combination depends on the circumstances at the time; it also affects the achievement of long-term objectives. Generally, heavy reliance on monetary policy will result in a lower rate of capital accumulation for growth but will aid the balance of payments. The structure of the economy may also be affected.

The potential effectiveness of any combination of policies aimed at managing the level of aggregate demand depends on an economy's Phillips Curve, the curve that shows what combinations of unemployment and price behavior an economy can actually achieve. The curve shows how close an economy comes to reconciling full employment and price stability, what the trade-offs are of one for the other, and hence what possibilities are open to general economic policy. One of the most pressing tasks for policy is to devise means to improve the Phillips Curve and hence to raise the feasible goals for fiscal and monetary policies.

Selected Readings

For more elaborate general treatments of public finance, see any of the good intermediate-level textbooks, as for example, John F. Due, *Government Finance*, 3rd ed. (Homewood, Ill.: Richard D. Irwin, Inc., 1963), and William J. Schultz and C. Lowell Harriss, *American Public Finance*, 8th ed. (Englewood Cliffs, N. J.: Prentice-Hall, Inc., 1965). Also see the book of readings, *Public Finance and Fiscal Policy*, J. Scherer and J. A. Papke, eds. (Boston: Houghton Mifflin Company, 1966).

For a full and authoritative account of the theoretical aspects of public finance, see Richard A. Musgrave, *The Theory of Public Finance* (New York: McGraw-Hill Book Company, 1959). This is an advanced and difficult treatise.

On public expenditures, see Jesse Burkhead and Jerry Miner, *Public Expenditure* (Chicago: Aldine, 1971). The best book on promoting efficiency in the public sector remains Charles J. Hitch and Roland N. McKean, *The Economics of Defense in the Nuclear Age* (Cambridge: Harvard University Press, 1960). John K. Galbraith's famous *The Affluent Society*, 2nd ed. (Boston: Houghton Mifflin Company, 1971), presents the argument that the quality of public services in the U.S. is too low.

The single most informative source is *The Budget of the United States Government*, which appears annually and neatly summarizes the president's expenditure policies, both in the aggregate and for each program. An invaluable discussion of the major issues in the budget is found in the annual series published by The Brookings Institution, *Setting National Priorities*, 1971–, by C. L. Schultze and others.

On the problems of state and local governments, see Werner Z. Hirsch, *The Economics of State and Local Government* (New York: McGraw-Hill Book Company, 1970). Also valuable are the *Reports of the Advisory Commission on Intergovernmental Relations* (Washington, D. C.: Superintendent of Documents). Also see D. Netzer, *Economics of the Property Tax* (Washington, D. C.: The Brookings Institution, 1966).

On metropolitan areas, see the book of readings, *Economics of Metropolitan Areas*, ed. Benjamin Chinitz (Englewood Cliffs, N. J.: Prentice-Hall, Inc., 1964).

The literature on the economics of taxation is enormous. On questions of equity, the fundamental source remains Henry C. Simons, *Personal Income Taxation* (Chicago: University of Chicago Press, 1938). Contemporary views on issues of tax policy can be found in Joseph A. Pechman, *Federal Tax Policy*, rev. ed. (Washington, D. C.: The Brookings Institution, 1971), and in Lester C. Thurow, *The Impact of Taxes on the American Economy* (New York: Frederick A. Praeger, Inc., 1971). Also see R. Goode, *The Individual Income Tax* (Washington, D. C.: The Brookings Institution, 1964), and C. S. Shoup, *Federal Estate and Gift Taxes* (Washington, D. C.: The Brookings Institution, 1966). For studies of the economic effects of the tax system, see the references in Chapter Six. On the issues of excessive income taxation, see *The Role of Direct and Indirect Taxes in the Federal Revenue System*, A Conference Report of the National Bureau of Economic Research and The Brookings Institution (Princeton: Princeton University Press, 1964).

For a full discussion of the negative income tax, see Christopher Green, *Negative Taxes and The Poverty Problem* (Washington, D. C.: The Brookings Institution, 1967). Fiscal policy is discussed in Walter W. Heller, *New Dimensions of Political Economy* (Cambridge: Harvard University Press, 1966), and Arthur Okun, *The Political Economy of Prosperity* (Washington, D. C.: The Brookings Institution, 1970). Also see the *Annual Reports of the Council of Economic Advisers* (Washington, D. C.: Superintendent of Documents).

INDEX

131